SCHOOL SMART

Make Your Child A Success

Steven Hastings

First published in Great Britain in 2007 by
Virgin Books Ltd
Thames Wharf Studios
Rainville Road
London
W6 9HA

A catalogue record for this book is available from the British
Library.

ISBN 978 0 7535 1229 6

The paper used in this book is a natural, recyclable product
made from wood grown in sustainable forests. The
manufacturing process conforms to the regulations of the
country of origin.

Typeset by Phoenix Photosetting, Chatham, Kent
Printed and bound in Great Britain by
CPI Bookmarque, Croydon, CR0 4TD

CONTENTS

INTRODUCTION

Forty years ago it was common for schools to have a sign on the gates saying NO PARENTS BEYOND THIS POINT. It wasn't a health and safety issue. It was a statement of intent. There was school and there was life outside school. And they were two very separate things. Educating children was the job of teachers. PARENTS KEEP OUT.

Today, it's different. Learning doesn't stop at the school gates. Education has become a partnership between parents, schools and young people themselves. And that's a good thing. But it also means that parents are under more pressure than ever before, to understand and take part in an area of their child's upbringing that would once have been left to the professionals.

Today, if a child struggles at school, then the parents are held to be somehow responsible, alongside the teachers. It doesn't take a great leap of imagination to envisage the possibility of Ofsted sending inspectors into our homes, in case Mum and Dad need putting into special measures. It's understandable if some parents feel anxious and confused about their role.

Everybody wants to help their child learn, and to help them succeed. But that's easier said than done. Your own experience of school was probably very different to your child's experience. The educational landscape is changing. Take the small matter of choosing a school for your child. Parents are cast as consumers, but are sometimes uncertain about what should be on their shopping list. Academies? Specialist colleges? Faith schools? The choice can be bewildering.

The same is true when it comes to helping children with their learning. Parents want to be involved, but aren't always sure of the right moves. They don't want to be pushy parents, but they feel under pressure to do *something*. To be involved. Like small children running round a football field, chasing the ball, their efforts can be frantic, but counterproductive.

School Smart seeks to offer guidance and reassurance. How you raise your child is, of course, a matter of personal choice. Something that comes from within, not from the pages of a book. And *School Smart* doesn't set out to be a parenting manual in the widest sense. Its remit is simple, and narrow – to help you to help your child become an effective learner. But because good learning involves a holistic approach the book strays into broader areas, such as the importance of sleep, exercise and diet. Hopefully, it manages to do so without being patronising or overprescriptive.

Inevitably, this kind of book has to cover a wide range of topics, each an area of research and debate in its own right. There are whole works devoted to child nutrition, teaching children to read or improving their memory. *School Smart* is about the bigger picture. It's about how these different parts of the jigsaw might fit together and how, once they are fitted together, they might offer a coherent approach to helping children become effective learners.

This is an exciting time in the field of learning. There's a growing interest in the way young people study, and what they should be studying. Neuroscientists are discovering more about how the brain receives and processes information. Psychologists are showing that success at school doesn't depend just on intelligence, but on a whole range of other factors, such as happiness and self-esteem. Educationists are emphasising the need to turn young people into flexible thinkers who will flourish in a complex, rapidly changing world.

School Smart is an attempt to bring these different strands together, and offer parents an overview. You aren't just *a* partner in your child's education. You are the senior partner. It is parents, not teachers, who are best placed to fill children with a love of learning and a spirit of enquiry. Even the most progressive schools find their good intentions can be shunted aside by the pressure of league tables and the curriculum. *School Smart* is about helping your child to do well at school. That means learning how to 'play the game'. Getting results. But it's also about helping your child become a creative and well-rounded thinker, who will thrive in the classroom and beyond.

Part I

SMART THINKING

1. UNRAVELLING INTELLIGENCE: YOUR CHILD'S BRAIN AND HOW IT MIGHT WORK

Kim's friends think she's 'brainy'. She answers questions in class and gets good marks for her homework. She understands fractions, can string sentences together in French and won a school prize for an art project. 'Brainy' is their word – but is it the right word? Just how much of Kim's success is to do with her brain?

This book isn't about pushy parenting, or hothousing, or turning your child into a genius. But it does argue that you can make a difference. This means tackling all kinds of things: wellbeing, self-esteem, attitudes to learning, and how well your child is taught, nurtured and supported. It's not just about your child's brain. But when you're talking about education – and when you're trying to make the most of your child's 'natural' intelligence – it's worth taking a moment to find out the basics of how the brain learns.

ABOUT THE BRAIN

Brains change. Your brain is not the same today as it was yesterday. It's certainly not the same as it was a year ago, or ten years ago. Most of us, if we stop to reflect, are aware of this. Tasks we found easy a decade ago, we now find taxing. Things that once vexed us, we now find easy. Just like our muscles, our brain gets stronger the more we use it and challenge it. If we neglect it, it may grow weaker.

Babies are born with almost as many brain cells as they are ever likely to have – around a hundred billion of them. But those cells don't work in isolation. There is an unimaginably complex network of connections between the cells that allows electrical impulses to travel through the brain. During childhood that network of connections is growing and expanding every day. Some of this growth is determined by our DNA, the genetic code that makes us uniquely who we are. But our brains are also shaped by the world around us, by the things we see and do, and hear and feel. In response to our experiences, new connections are made, old ones are strengthened or weakened. Some cells, which aren't stimulated, will die. Others will form thousands of links. By the time we reach adulthood, there will be over a hundred trillion constantly changing connections between our brain cells.

Each person's brain is unique, because each person's life is also unique. The brain is not a computer; it's a living thing. It becomes suited to our purpose. Biologically speaking, its purpose is to ensure our survival. So the brain modifies its structure in response to the different tasks it is required to do. It establishes the neural connections needed to meet particular challenges. The more we use certain parts of our brain, the more developed and efficient those parts of the brain become. The well-trodden pathways are the ones that become strongest. In an actor, the parts of the brain responsible for language and speech may be larger than average. In a taxi driver, it's the area dealing with directions and spatial memory that is likely to be more highly developed. And so it goes on. Practice makes perfect – because practice changes the brain.

Think of the neural network as a series of paths in the local park. If a pathway is well trodden it is quicker and easier to walk along it. Eventually, perhaps, a man from the council comes along and slaps down some tarmac, turning the path into something more permanent. It's like that in the brain. Some neural pathways become so well trodden that they will always be there, even if they aren't used for several years.

There's some evidence that when the brain is faced with new experiences it recruits brain cells from other areas to help it meet the challenge. It calls in reinforcements. Once the new task becomes automatic, it requires fewer cells and the reinforcements can be freed up for other work. In this way, different networks are constantly competing against each other. Those that are most in use become strong while others have some of their cells stolen and so become weaker. The brain begins to rationalise itself, cutting back those connections not in use so as to be able to concentrate its resources on the more active areas. It's a sort of fine-tuning process. It means that ultimately there are fewer connections, but the connections that remain are stronger and more stable.

This ability of the brain to change and adapt is known as plasticity. And it's good news, because it means that our minds are flexible. It means that we can learn. It means that your child's educational journey can be an adventure.

Did You Know?

- The average adult human brain contains around 100 billion neurons. These make up the 'grey matter' of the brain. There are also billions more cells known as 'glial cells', which act as supporting structure. But it's the neurons that are responsible for mental activity.
- Each neuron has a main fibre known as the axon, which transmits electrical impulses. And each neuron

has many smaller branches known as dendrites, which receive electrical impulses from other neurons. The point at which the dendrite of one neuron meets the axon of another is known as a synapse.

- A neuron may have up to 10,000 synaptic connections with other neurons.

- Between birth and puberty the number of synapses in the brain increases, but around puberty the number dips, as the brain starts to lose connections that aren't well used.

- Many axons are coated in a myelin sheath, which acts as a kind of insulation and allows messages to be sent more quickly. The building up of myelin is thought to continue throughout the first twenty or so years of our life.

SHAPING YOUR CHILD'S BRAIN

Scientists used to think that the first few years of a child's life were critical to the development of the brain. After that, they argued, the basic architecture was firmly in place. The brain was hard-wired. But current thinking suggests that our brain cells go on making new connections at an impressive rate until well into our teenage years. Even after that, our neural network continues to evolve right though our lives, though changes become more subtle. It's a shifting landscape, a heaving city, in which some buildings are torn down, and others put up overnight.

But can you directly alter the way your child's brain develops? Of course you can. We all know that a mother's behaviour and lifestyle during pregnancy will have an impact on her child's brain even before birth. We all know that from the moment a baby is born, the influence of parents is crucial. The brain is partly a product of its environment, and parents are uniquely placed to decide what sort of environment a child grows up in.

But when it comes to actually making your child brighter, or more creative, or a better learner, things are not so clear cut. We've already seen that challenging the brain expands the number of neural connections and hard-wires them into its structure. So, in theory, the more challenges we face, the more strong connections we should have, and the smarter we should become. For this reason, some experts support the idea of 'enrichment'. They suggest we should control children's surroundings in a very specific way, introducing them to specific activities at different points of their development, in order to stimulate the growth of the neural connections in the brain. And to back this up, they give examples of times when the brain seems particularly receptive to learning particular skills: for example, young children seem to find language learning easier than adults.

It's certainly true that the experiences we give our children shape the way they think and learn. When we teach a child to read or to write, we are changing the architecture of his brain for ever. But we just don't know enough about how the brain works to devise some magical kind of brain-based learning that will turn all children into high achievers. Every individual brain is different. And there's no real evidence that speeding up children's development will, in any meaningful way, make them more clever or successful in the long term. It may just get you caught up in some kind of exhausting and confusing race – who will be the first to talk, to read, to reach the level required for their SATs? – that turns out to be pointless. Worse still, it's quite possible that pushing children to achieve new skills before they are ready could have an adverse effect on their long-term learning.

So while the principle of enrichment can sound reassuring to parents keen to get stuck in and make a difference, the idea of providing wall-to-wall challenges for your child should be treated with some caution. It's certainly not helpful if it makes you feel guilty or under pressure to provide constant stimulation. Relax. In the right surroundings a child's brain just can't help but learn. Childhood is a naturally rich time. Children can have freedom and fun, and still develop at their own pace. And they can be stimulated, challenged and instructed. Playing with a selection of toys, engaging in a healthy variety of activities, spending time with a range of adults and other children; these things are enough. All of them will stimulate a child's mind and help with the development of his brain. And all of them will be explored more fully later in this book.

BRAIN SCIENCE AND LEARNING

The human brain is nature's most remarkable achievement. It is complex, mysterious and sophisticated, and most scientists will happily admit that our understanding of it is limited. Limited, but improving all the time.

We know more about the brain than ever before, and it would be foolish to ignore that. There's no doubt that research into the brain can have implications for how we raise and educate children. But raising a smart child isn't just about science. It's also about instinct, common sense and a human understanding of what makes people tick. And there's a danger that getting too caught up in the latest theories can be counterproductive. We all know that science moves on quickly. Each year, new discoveries roll off the academic presses. Old findings are put through the shredder. And that's why understanding the brain, and writing about it, is a tricky business. If we get too closely involved with particular theories, we can easily find ourselves being led up the well-trodden, neurally robust garden path. Today's facts can turn out to be tomorrow's fiction.

Ten years ago there was a lot of talk of the importance of right-brain and left-brain thinking. It was thought that the left side of the brain dealt with logic and reasoning, while the right side was responsible for creativity and intuition. There were suggestions that if we could determine whether children were predominantly right- or left-brained, we would know where their strengths and weakness lay. We might even be able to put them on the appropriate career path. That kind of thinking is now well out of date. It's true that different parts of the brain have specialised jobs. But the left-side, right-side model appears to have been a gross oversimplification. The workings of our brains are hugely complex and even the simplest tasks usually involve both sides of our brain working together.

It's a good example of how it's possible to oversimplify. Another example is the idea, popularised in countless self-help manuals, that we only use 10 per cent of our brains. Serious scientists dismiss that as ridiculous. Our brains are being used even as we breathe, eat or sleep. The idea that our minds have enormous untapped potential may well be correct. But expressing this as a simple percentage, or suggesting that somehow part of our brain is simply switched off and put into storage, is nonsense.

Similarly controversial ideas have been applied to education and learning. In recent years, there have been a number of brain-based theories that have claimed to explain the way children learn, and to offer ways of helping them learn better. One of these is the theory of something called 'learning styles' – the suggestion that different children learn in different ways. It sounds simple and logical. And it's an idea that has taken hold in schools up and down the country, and been promoted by the government as the VAK model of learning. VAK stands for visual, auditory and kinaesthetic. Put simply, the principle is that some children learn best through looking, others through listening and others through rolling up their sleeves and getting stuck in. Some schools have gone to town on it.

But is there any scientific basis to the idea? Yes and no. But mostly no. It's true that we probably all acquire certain preferences for how we like to learn. But this is largely a question of habit and familiarity. There's no scientific evidence that our brains are wired differently at birth, and that we're destined to fall into one or other of the three categories. There's no evidence that your child is naturally a visual learner, or an auditory one. And yet some schools design all their teaching around learning-styles theories, labelling children as a particular kind of learner, and then teaching them in the 'appropriate' way. And the labels may be more than a mental note in the teacher's mind. It may be recorded on your child's file notes, or it may even be written on a badge and stuck on his chest. Some teachers have been known to literally label children, getting them to wear stickers that say things like 'I'm a kinaesthetic learner'.

These kind of labels, whether they're pinned, stuck or noted, are bound to limit our view of any particular child and, perhaps more importantly, that child's view of his own abilities. The reality is that visual, auditory and kinaesthetic are not ways of learning – they are ways of receiving information. And the idea that we can receive new information in different ways is useful and interesting. But it's not the answer to the mysteries of the brain.

Good schools are aware of learning styles, but they don't base their whole teaching around the idea. If teachers include a 'seeing', 'hearing' and 'doing' element to every lesson then it's bound to be more interesting than if they just ramble on endlessly with their nose in a textbook. That's not neuroscience: it's just common sense. Good schools make children aware that there are different ways of learning, and that a good learner has to be able to learn in all those different ways. And that's healthy and positive. Good schools also think about the learning process from the child's perspective, and that too is a good thing. But getting hung up on the minutiae of learning styles is restrictive and inflexible. A broad-based holistic education should be, and needs to be, more than a single scientific theory.

Things To Do

- Find out if your child's school follows any 'brain' theories, such as VAK. You should find something on the website or in the prospectus, but if not, ask.
- Find out more about it. A good place to start is the website of the *Times Educational Supplement* (www.tes.co.uk) – most terms entered into the search engine throw up loads of reading.
- Look at latest thinking and what other schools are doing. Be critical. And if you feel your child is being shunted into something too limiting, think about using activities and discussions at home to help balance things out.

This doesn't mean you won't find plenty of brain science that is helpful and entertaining, and that provides some thought-provoking approaches to your child's learning. In particular, you may well find research that confirms and explains what you or your child's teacher has been thinking. This is when it gets really useful. If it helps you understand more fully what you have already been noticing for yourself, then it's a good place to start.

Here's one example: most people would say that a happy, well-balanced child is more likely to do well at school than one who is emotionally distressed. And science offers some answers as to why that might be. The brain is designed for survival, and so strong emotions take precedence over more trivial things such as history lessons. If we're anxious or frightened, then our brain will direct its energies to dealing with that, rather than worrying about French homework. In the short term, this may mean nothing more than being distracted and under par for a day or two. But long-term emotional stress can redirect so much neural energy that it hinders the development of certain parts of the brain, causing the death of neurons, and the pruning of connections between them.

And another example: parents and teachers would say that children learn best when they're motivated and can see the point of what they are doing. Well, this intuition is also well founded. Research shows that certain parts of the brain may become more developed and active when the information being processed has a direct application to our lives. Because our brains are dedicated to survival, it's only to be expected that they prioritise learning that is relevant.

And again: we all know that teenagers can be moody, difficult, disorganised and impulsive. Can it all be down to hormones? Only partly. It may also be that it's a time of great change in the prefrontal cortex, the part of the brain that deals with planning, self-awareness and decision-making. This part of the brain is slower to develop, and is still being reshaped and reorganised during our teenage years. It doesn't reach its adult state until our early twenties. So it's no surprise if during this period things can sometimes get a bit unpredictable.

Sometimes science tells us things we don't know. Sometimes it explains things we already know. We can't ignore it, but we should always bear in mind that neuroscience is still developing, and that our understanding of the brain is far from complete.

NATURE OR NURTURE?

A child's brain is shaped by his experiences. But it's also shaped by genetic factors. So to what extent is intelligence genetically determined? And to what extent is it the result of circumstances? How much difference can we really make?

Experts sometimes play the percentages game. The intelligence cocktail is two parts DNA to one part environment, they say. Or two parts environment to one part DNA. But it's a fruitless argument. Nature and nurture are so closely entwined that it's impossible to untangle them. Genes exist only within an environment. From the moment a child is conceived, nature and nurture are at work together. If a boy's dad is a keen mathematician, then it's likely that they'll play plenty of number games together. It would hardly be surprising if maths were then to be one of the boy's favourite subjects at school, and one he does particularly well in. Has he inherited a natural aptitude for figures? Quite possibly. Has he benefited from an appropriate role model and a daily dose of Sudoku? Almost certainly.

There are no hard-and-fast rules. From time to time a child prodigy comes along who seems to have a natural talent far beyond the normal. They may learn to play a musical instrument with hardly any instruction. In such a case, nature seems strong. Someone else may flourish later in life, as the result of years of persistence. In such a case, it's the environment that seems more powerful. Can you turn an average child into a genius? Probably not. With practice, we could all become better runners. We could get fitter, and run faster and further. Could we all run a marathon? Possibly. Could we all become Olympic athletes? Doubtful. There are limits to what we can achieve. But these limits may be far wider than we imagine.

There are so many factors at work. The physical development of the brain is shaped by a combination of genes and circumstance. The broad outline might be genetically determined, but it is life itself that colours in the detail. You can nurture your child's brain by giving them the sort of environment that stimulates development. But just as important as the physical make-up of the brain is the way that it will be used. And that too is a combination of nature and nurture: it depends on a child's personality, the way they are raised and taught, the choices they make and their own free will. And that's why this book takes a holistic approach. Because there's no other way.

Let's take one of the apparently simplest factors. Hard work. If you've got an average child, encouraging them to work hard will pay dividends. If you've got a bright child, a top-of-the-class achiever, then talent will carry them through. Right? One study, carried out at a music academy in Berlin, found that the students rated highest by their teachers were those who practised hardest. 'Superior' students were found to practise an average of twenty-four hours a week, while 'good' students practised an average of just nine hours a week. It's the same in many other walks of life. The people who achieve the most aren't always the cleverest, or the smartest. They're the most motivated, and the most focused. They work hard. They fulfil their potential.

There's no point in worrying about your child's genes. Or your own. There's not much you can do about them! As with most things in life, it's a question of making the most of what you've got. Better to focus on the things you can influence than the things you can't. Brains are like cars. Some are simply more powerful than others. But when it comes to getting from A to B, it's not just about the size of your engine. Every part of the car needs to be in good working order. You need a skilful driver, someone who can follow directions, choose the best route, avoid oncoming traffic. Someone who is going to put in the hours on the road. All you can do is to help your child maximise their abilities. Help them get that engine fine-tuned. Help them become a good driver.

JUDGING INTELLIGENCE

People value intelligence: they value it in partners, friends or employees. Indeed, we all make judgements about other people's intelligence on a daily basis. When we meet someone for the first time, consciously or subconsciously we form an opinion of how 'intelligent' they are. We rely on a mishmash of signs and signals: the clothes they wear, the way they speak, the words they use or the job they do. We make snap judgements based on a mixture of prejudice, instinct and guesswork. I once met a mother who had just come from an interview at a small private school. She had gone along with her seven-year-old daughter, who had been asked by the head teacher to spell the word 'office'. The girl was bright and conscientious, but nervous and not used to spelling out loud. She left out one 'f'. And the head teacher made a judgement about how intelligent the girl was, and how the school should treat her. Prejudice, instinct and guesswork.

Unfortunately, the same unreliable mix tends to be at work with more formal ways of measuring brain power. Take IQ tests. Thousands of people do. The tests ask you to complete sequences of numbers, or match up different shapes after they've been rotated through 90 degrees. Or pick out from a list of words the two that have the same meaning. For years people thought this was the best measure of a person's intelligence. There's even a club for people who are good at fitting shapes together: Mensa was founded in 1946 for those people whose IQ is in the top 2 per cent, and its 28,000 UK members include over 2,000 children.

Yet most IQ tests focus almost exclusively on numerical and verbal reasoning. Numbers. Words. Logic. And if you practised hard, you'd soon get better at taking this kind of test. Just as you'd get better at doing the daily crossword. So IQ tests tell us something about children's abilities, but only in a very simplistic way.

Another popular benchmark of intelligence is success in exams. But what do exams measure? Well, most of the time, they measure very specific things. What you remember about photosynthesis. Enzymes. Peter the Great. In short, 'How much stuff do you know?' They're a pretty good test of your memory, and your ability to write quickly for a couple of hours without your hand cramping up. But do they measure intelligence?

When it comes to spotting children who might have particular gifts or talents, common sense and observation are probably more use than diagnostic tests. It's not an exact science. Children reveal their talents in different ways and at different times. Gifted children are often very articulate. They may do very well at school and be hard-working and ahead of their class. They may be popular and relate well to their friends. They may be curious, constantly asking their teacher questions. They may even do very well at IQ tests.

Or they could be completely different. They may do badly at school, because they find it boring. They may become rebellious and disinterested. They may not enjoy spending time with other children because they find them immature. Instead they might spend time alone or with adults. They may have very strong views and opinions and always get into arguments. They may take an unusual approach to life – and may even seem a little strange.

It's important to remember that all children are unique and that sticking general labels on them is rarely very helpful. Even if that label is a shiny gold star that says 'talented'.

Did You Know?

- In the early 1800s phrenology was a popular science. It was thought that by measuring a person's head, and feeling out all its dents and bumps, it was possible to find out how intelligent they were.
- The type of questions asked in IQ tests were developed in the early 1900s by Alfred Binet, a French psychologist. They were designed to highlight children who might face difficulties at school.
- In the 1920s, Lewis H Terman, of Stanford University, began a piece of research intended to show that people's station in life was determined by their IQ. He got a nasty shock when he found that a group of tramps, picked at random off the streets, had higher IQs than a bunch of New York cops.

WHAT IS INTELLIGENCE?

The problem with measuring intelligence is that no one's quite sure how to define exactly what intelligence is in the first place.

It's clearly about more than remembering a set of facts for exams, but what else is it? Being able to think around a problem? Having the right words in the right situation? Being good at chess? Not surprisingly, the puzzle has bothered scientists for some time. After all, finding the key to cleverness would be a major, and very lucrative, breakthrough.

The first person to claim to have found the magic answer was Charles Spearman, an English psychologist. His experiments in the early twentieth century found that people who did well in a variety of different tests were all using the same part of their brain – the lateral prefrontal cortex, as we now call it. Back then, Spearman just called it 'g'.

This 'g' was identified by Spearman and his followers as the hard drive of the brain. It indicated something called general intelligence. Which meant that if you were smart in one way then you were likely to be smart in other ways too. If you could juggle quadratic equations then you could probably understand the politics of the French Revolution and play a decent game of draughts.

But the theory of general intelligence doesn't explain why some people write nice poetry, but can't do simple sums. These people bugged Howard Gardner, a professor at Harvard University – or rather, their existence bugged him. And in 1983, he published work that suggested cleverness was more complex – and clever – than Spearman had claimed. He came up with a theory of multiple intelligences.

Gardner's theory categorised skills into different groups and put each of these groups under the control of dedicated and distinct neural pathways. Rather than everything falling under the control of one superpower, big g, different skills come under the control of different individual intelligences.

In all, Gardner suggested there were actually seven types of intelligence: linguistic, logical–mathematical, bodily–kinaesthetic, musical, interpersonal, intrapersonal and spatial. In simple terms these mean you can be good with words, good with figures, good with your body, good at music, good with people, or good at sitting in a corner and thinking deeply about the meaning of life. Spatial intelligence is harder to explain – it's the kind of abstract intelligence shown by architects or sculptors, who have an awareness of how their work fits into a wider space. Gardner has since added an eighth intelligence to the list – naturalist intelligence – that describes the way in which we relate to the natural world. He also proposes many sub-intelligences within each of his categories. Indeed some scientists have gone as far as to list a hundred or more different intelligences.

The idea of multiple intelligences is appealing. It seems to confirm what we already know. People can be good at some things, but not others. 'That Wayne Rooney,' says the man at the bus stop. 'Bloody genius.' 'Yeah,' says his mate. 'Thick as two short planks, though.'

And it makes sense. We know what they mean. Brilliant at football – unlikely to find a cure for cancer.

In many ways the idea of multiple intelligences is as much about semantics as science. It's just asking us to rethink how we use the word 'intelligence'. Whereas we might say someone good at maths is intelligent, we would probably say someone good at sport or dancing is merely 'talented'. Society still values their abilities. Great dancers or sports players can earn more money than a great mathematician. But we just don't think of their abilities as 'intelligence' – even if we do use the word 'genius' from time to time. What Gardner does is encourage us to think of intelligence in a wider, more flexible, sense.

Rightly or wrongly, few people do. Since the Middle Ages the intelligences most highly valued in schools have been linguistic and logical–mathematical intelligence. Even today, if children take a GCSE in Physical Education, they have to sit a written paper. We can't quite bring ourselves to give an 'academic' qualification to someone just for running round a sports hall, however well they do it.

2. HELPING CREATIVITY HAPPEN: HOW TO NURTURE A CREATIVE CHILD

Sam can't sing, has two left feet, draws cows that look like buses and can't stand the thought of poetry. So how on earth will she ever get a kick out of being creative? Maybe it's time to think outside the box!

Creativity is about an approach to life and learning, not about making masterpieces. And it can go a long way to making your child happier and more successful at school.

WHAT IS CREATIVITY?

If you ask most people to define creativity, they'll probably mention writing, painting or music. If you ask them to give you an example of a creative person, they'll probably come up with big names like Mozart, Picasso or Shakespeare.

Many of us are programmed to connect creativity with making works of art. We think of it like inspiration: something materialising out of the blue to give us the key to a catchy tune or a word to rhyme with 'caterpillar'. But there are plenty of examples of creativity outside the arts. Discovering the theory of relativity? Cracking the genome code? Tackling global warming? Anything that makes a difference is likely to be the product of some pretty creative thinking.

And for those of us unlikely to change the world, there's good news. Creativity isn't about greatness or genius. It's a mistake to think it's the preserve of a few very clever, very special people. It's a mistake to think that because your child prefers ping-pong to painting they'll never be creative. Because being creative is something we all do, each and every day. Every time we solve a problem, every time we tell a lie or tell a story to a friend, every time we daydream or imagine. Creativity is about having thoughts and ideas. It's about being curious about how things work. It's about coming up with solutions. It's also about being original. And since each of us is unique, being original really means just being ourselves. So everybody is creative.

But as we get older, our levels of creativity, like some of our more fleshy features, can start to drop. It's understandable. At work, most of us do the same tasks day in, day out. At home we watch the same programmes, play the same games, have the same conversations. Over and over. They become routine. They become easy and familiar and comforting. We fall back on what we know, rather than bothering to come up with new ideas. We lose our sense of adventure, and happily plump for the safe options.

Fortunately, children are different. They see the world through fresh, new eyes and then they use what they see in original ways. They love fantasy and play. They tend to enjoy meeting new people. They get excited by new ideas. They have wonderful imaginations. And because of all that, creativity comes naturally to them. Just think of the way young children use language. You won't hear them talking in clichés. Instead, they'll use expressions that they've made up themselves, to try to explain what they are thinking, expressions that sound new and fresh, almost poetic.

In the adult world, we tend to look for an end product to people's creativity. So if someone invents a new kind of vacuum cleaner or writes a bestselling novel we would say they are creative. A nine-year-old child is unlikely to do either of those things. With children, it's more useful to think of creativity as a way of working. If they're coming up with ideas, if they're constantly exploring and trying new things, then they are being creative.

Did You Know?

- The Tokyo-based think-tank, the Nomura Institute, believes the development of human society has evolved through four 'ages'. We have passed through the age of agriculture, the age of industry and the age of information. Now we are entering the age of creativity.
- A 2003 Ofsted survey of 42 schools found that one in five was 'exceptionally good' at promoting creativity.
- However, there is far less emphasis on creative development within our national guidelines than in many other countries. In Singapore, Hong Kong and the Republic of Korea, for example, creative thinking is seen as the bedrock on which the whole of learning is based.

While we're trying to explain what creativity is, it's also worth trying to explain what it is not.

Creativity isn't the same thing as academic ability. In fact, creative children often fare badly in exams. Nor is it the same thing as talent. It's possible to be a talented carpenter, for example, without being particularly creative. And being creative doesn't mean being undisciplined, or badly behaved. Admittedly, research shows that children who are labelled 'creative' have a higher-than-average chance of getting into trouble at school. And it's true that arguing with the teacher, shouting out impulsively and refusing to let an issue drop are all signs of awakening creativity – and may not go down too well in the classroom. But real creativity needs focus, concentration and persistence.

When I was teaching there were plenty of parents who explained their son's or daughter's poor behaviour by saying, 'Oh, there's nothing we can do, he (or she) is very creative.' And since I'd never want to stifle creativity, I often just nodded sagely in agreement. But most of these parents were making excuses for naughtiness. The most creative work in the class was almost always done by motivated, well-organised pupils who responded well in lessons, related successfully with their peers and channelled their abilities and energies effectively.

WHY DOES CREATIVITY MATTER?

Creativity is a highly marketable commodity. In a rapidly changing world, the ability to be creative is a valuable asset. It can open doors. It can make money. The 'creative industries' are the fastest-growing part of the British economy. They employ around 1.4 million people and contribute more than £100 billion each year to the UK economy. But it's not just about TV, advertising and film; even traditional businesses are putting an increased emphasis on creative thinking. It crops up in job interviews, training programmes and performance-related pay scales from the shop floor to the glass ceiling. It can be just as important, and rewarding, to be creative in the cement industry as in the music industry.

In a recent survey by the Work Foundation, corporate bosses identified 'recruiting and managing creative employees' as one of the five key factors for business success. And that's unlikely to change. The rapid progress of technology means children have to be flexible and have to be prepared to think creatively about the future. It's estimated that 60 per cent of the jobs that today's primary children will do have not yet been invented. That's a staggering thought. It means that a great deal of the knowledge children learn in school may not actually be much use to them. In fact it may not be of any use at all. But if they learn to be creative, to be flexible and freethinking, then they will be able to adapt more easily as the world changes around them.

And creativity isn't just about job prospects. Creative people are more likely to be able to express their feelings. They find it easier to overcome problems in life, as well as in the workplace. They are more likely to engage with their surroundings and with other people. A creative child is a happy child, and a happy child is very likely to become a contented adult.

Did You Know?

- When it comes to creative problem-solving, experts identify two types of thinkers – convergent and divergent. Divergent thinkers let their imaginations take hold and produce lots of different ideas and possibilities. Convergent thinkers can analyse these possible solutions and narrow them down to the most suitable solution. The most successful creative people are those that are skilled in both types of thinking.

HOW *NOT* TO MAKE YOUR CHILD *UN*CREATIVE

Encouraging creativity is important. But since all children are naturally creative, perhaps the really important thing is to give them a chance to use it without them feeling stifled or undermined by the adults around them.

Schools don't always foster creativity as they should. Most of them will talk about creativity. They've probably got the jargon at their fingertips. You may even see it in the prospectus or on the website. And there is some good work being done: some schools have special project weeks, where children are allowed to pursue their own ideas, without too much interference from the teachers. Others have writers or artists 'in residence' – people who make a living out of being creative, and who can inspire children to try new things.

But when it comes down to it, on a daily basis, it can be a different story. Teachers often find it difficult to give children the freedom to follow their instincts. There's the curriculum to follow. There's the looming shadow of tests and examinations. And there's the structure of the school day, with its bells and breaks. Many, many times I've watched excellent lessons where the class has been absorbed in creative tasks, engrossed even. Then the bell rings and everyone has to move on.

It's probably not surprising that research has found the sharpest drop in children's natural creativity is between the ages of five and six – or when they first go to school.

Things (Not) To Do

- One of the keys to being creative is to do something for its own sake, because you enjoy it. If you push your children to do things they don't want to do, then they're unlikely to be creative, however creative the activity.
- With younger children, the point of an activity is often the 'doing' of it, rather than the end product. Don't fall into the adult habit of passing judgement on what they achieve.
- Some activities are designed to keep young children quiet, rather than to stimulate their creativity. Try not to fall into this trap more than necessary. Colouring books or join-the-dots may keep children occupied, but they don't promote creativity in the same way as a blank sheet of paper and a pot of paint.

As children get older the pressures on creativity can come from all sides. Parents and teachers want them to start producing 'proper' work. Their friends want them to look, sound and act a certain way. They may be feeling confused and insecure. So creativity can take another hit.

At this stage in particular, it can be the home environment that offers the safe space for letting children explore their creative urges. Even so, there are pitfalls. And the most well-intentioned parents are sometimes the worst culprits when it comes to stifling creativity. Not many of us can be creative on demand. Not many of us feel like experimenting with something crazy if we think someone might be watching. It's possible for parents to take too much interest. If your child feels like they're under surveillance, then they're unlikely to be at their most creative. Give them space!

And, while it's good to offer praise, it's important not to be too judgemental. At school, almost everything your son or daughter does will be commented upon, marked or graded. Every sum and sentence will be evaluated; every idea they try to articulate will be discussed, debated and challenged. This creates pressure: pressure to do what the teacher wants, pressure to produce something that will meet with approval, a shiny star or a nice 'A' grade. But creativity is about trying out new things. It's about taking a gamble. It's about doing what you want to do, not what other people say you should be doing. And it's about failure. Creative people don't come up with brilliant idea after brilliant idea. Most of the time they fail. They fail better. Then they succeed. But too many children are afraid of failure. That means they are afraid to take risks. And you can't be creative if you don't take risks.

CREATIVE ENCOURAGEMENT

Suppose your child draws a picture. Suppose you don't like it. It looks to you like childish scribbling. It looks like the last one they drew, which you have stuck on the fridge. And like the one before that, which is pinned to the back of the bedroom door. And the one before that on the toilet wall. And the one before that . . .

There's a temptation to try to push them in a different direction. There's a temptation to encourage them to move on, to do something more 'grown-up'. But it's very important that children have some time to explore their creative instincts, without always having an adult say, 'That's good' or 'I don't like that'. Later on, the child will start to explore different ways of drawing, in their own time and in their own style. Or they may move on very quickly to building models or making machines and hardly ever bother with drawing again. But that 'childish' scribbling is an important part of their development.

It's creative.

Of course, there are times when children should be given set tasks, with rules and guidelines to be followed. This is all part of learning. But even then it's important to be flexible. I recall teaching a boy of twelve, who liked writing science-fiction stories. They were excellent – well written and highly inventive. He had a good eye for four-headed, many-clawed monsters from outer space. But his mother came to see me. 'Isn't there something we could do,' she asked, 'to stop him writing these stories?' They were about aliens, spaceships and people who travelled through time. She found them embarrassing. It wasn't the sort of thing she liked. And she pointed out that other people's children had 'grown out of all that'.

I tried to explain to her that if everyone 'grew out of' writing science fiction, there would be no science-fiction books, selling thousands of copies a year. No popular science-fiction TV series or films, watched by millions. I said that I would happily encourage her son to try writing different kinds of stories from time to time – but I certainly wasn't going to tell him he had to stop writing science fiction. And when the boy finally left school and went on to university, he did very well indeed. He achieved excellent A levels and went on to do a degree in physics. He did a lot of work about space, and when he graduated he specialised in astrophysics. He now studies black holes and contributes to our understanding of how the universe works. He probably still writes a bit of science fiction, for fun.

The problem is that success at school is often measured by a sense of 'growing up'. GCSE English questions, for example, are very grown-up indeed. Describe a perfect holiday. Write a letter complaining about a faulty toaster. Not many extra marks for extraterrestrials. And so parents, understandably, can feel uncomfortable if they think their child is stuck in 'babyish' habits, even if these are harmless – or creative. Or they may get hung up about proving how quickly their child is developing. We hear parents boasting all too often that their child has a higher reading age than others in the class, for example, or that they're doing work that most children don't normally do until the year above. If that happens naturally, then all well and good. But I've known parents discourage their children from reading a particular book, and push them to try something more demanding. Very often, the child doesn't enjoy the new book – it's too difficult. The result? Less enthusiasm for books. Less creativity.

MAKING YOUR HOME MORE CREATIVE

If you want to make your home a hotbed of creativity, then the best way is to lead by example. If you show your child that you enjoy creative activities, then they're more likely to follow suit. That doesn't mean you have to take up piano lessons – just that you should be curious about the world, and adventurous in your approach to everything from cooking in the kitchen to redecorating the front room. But yes, if you want to paint pictures or write poetry, then don't do it in secret or only after the children have gone to bed. Be proud of your creativity.

Things To Do

Playing games and telling stories are two of the best ways of freeing up the imagination and boosting creativity. Here are a few ideas.

How many things?

All you have to do is list as many things as you can in a certain category. But you get extra points if you come up with ideas that no one else gets. So it pays to be imaginative. For example, how many things can you think of that are red? 'Blood' isn't so imaginative. 'Cold hands' is more imaginative. 'Anger' is very imaginative.

How many uses?

A similar game, but this time you have to try to think of unusual uses for an everyday object. For example, how many uses can you think of for a brick? 'Building a house' isn't so imaginative. 'Using it as a doorstop' is more imaginative. 'Heating it up in a fire then frying an egg on it' is very imaginative.

Word Association

One person says two words that are connected in some way. The next person repeats the second of the two words and adds the next word that pops into their head. And so it goes on – perhaps something like this: *Dog-cat . . . cat-mouse . . . mouse-trap . . . trap-door . . . door-open . . . open-shut . . . shut-mouth . . . mouth-teeth . . . teeth-dentist . . . dentist-doctor . . .* and so on. You must say the first thing that comes into your head, however silly it sounds. If you start to 'block', that is to change your mind, or reject the first thing that you think of and choose something else, then you lose the game. Playing regularly will help you to be spontaneous.

Shared story-telling
Two or more people tell a story by taking it in turns. Each person adds a little bit to the story, then someone else takes a go. You add a sentence each, or even just a word at a time. The secret is to let your imagination run free, and try not to think too hard.

If you want a creative atmosphere at home, then you may need to lighten up. Creativity can be messy. Arts activities like drawing, painting and making models are always likely to lead to spilled paint or glue on the floor. Science experiments can be good for flashes and bangs.

It's important to have rules, and for children to learn to tidy up after themselves. But try not to be too obsessive about things always being neat, or try to find at least one area that can be given over to creative mess-making activities. Children need to feel that you are comfortable with what they are doing, not just tolerating it. They need to feel they can relax and take their time. I've seen some parents who tidy up as soon as their child loses interest in what they're doing. But children have short concentration spans. They sometimes need a break, but then they'll come back later and pick up where they left off. It might be hours later, or even days. Sometimes you just have to leave things lying around – and live with the mess!

And you need to be broad-minded. Creativity can be shocking. Creative ideas can be spontaneous and impulsive and disturbing. You may find you don't always like the direction your child's creativity is taking them. Perhaps they make up jokes or stories that you find inappropriate. Perhaps they express themselves by swearing or using rude words. Perhaps they find humour in situations that a grown-up sees as serious.

This is a difficult area – and ultimately parents must make their own choices about what they find acceptable. But try not to be too authoritarian. As adults we're able to censor our speech and actions. We don't always say what we are thinking, or do what we'd most like to do. We accept social rules and moderate our behaviour accordingly. Children and young adults need to learn these social rules, but they also need to be allowed to express themselves. Creativity is about pushing at boundaries and rules. If your child argues with you, they're being creative. If they lie to you, they're being creative. If they make an excuse not to do the housework, they're being creative. That doesn't mean these things are acceptable, but there are times when it's worth being a little tolerant.

And when you are laying down the rules – whether they're about neatness or behaviour – try to keep them simple and clear. Present them as part of a 'value system'. Explain that you have rules because it's important to be considerate of other people's feelings. But try to be the sort of parent who says 'yes', at least some of the time. If your child wants to do something, try to make it possible, rather than pointing out potential problems. If they have a particular passion, try to build on that.

Things To Do

Older children often worry that they're not creative or imaginative – even though they are usually *very* creative. Here are some ways of helping children see that they're creative.

Dream diary
Encourage your son or daughter to keep a record of their dreams in a private notebook. It will act as a reminder that their head is full of amazing stories and adventures. It's just a question of learning to access that imagination.

Hot seating
One person imagines they are a character, someone other than themselves. To help them a second person asks them

questions about their imaginary life. How old are they? Where do they live? What's their favourite hobby? Before long they will have created a character completely different to themselves, just by answering the questions imaginatively.

What if . . .
Asking children 'What if . . .' questions helps develop their imaginations. What if there was no gravity? What if there was no electricity? What if it was possible for people to fly?

Good things
There are lots of useful props that encourage children to be creative. Chemistry sets, clothes for dressing up, paint pots and brushes, musical instruments – the list is endless, of course. For older children, one of the surest ways of getting creative juices flowing is to let them loose with a camera or camcorder.

HELPING YOUR CHILD STAY CREATIVE

Allow your child plenty of time for unstructured play. This is important, whatever their age. Depending on how old they are, of course, play will take different forms: running, chasing, pretending, making. It may even look like daydreaming. But just because you've spent a lot of money buying 'educational' board games or expert sports equipment, it shouldn't mean there's no room for messing around with a cardboard box or a few sticks. The strength of children's imagination is such that they can find fun in almost anything. Try to see things from their point of view – not your own.

With younger children, try to comment on the process of doing something rather than the end product. It's all too easy to fall into the habit of praising everything they create, but this can make them feel that something is only worthwhile if they get something obviously 'good' at the end of it. If they learn to believe in the process itself as valuable, then they'll find it easier to experiment later on. Comments such as 'that looked fun', or 'you really enjoyed that, didn't you?' can be more useful than saying that what they have made, painted or written is good, bad or indifferent.

As children get older, it's particularly important to let them know you are on their side with this. Be reassuring. It's all too easy for children to feel under pressure from their friends, and to feel they have to be interested in the same things as everyone else. Let them know it's OK to daydream, to play out make-beliefs, to have imaginary friends, to think things other people don't think. And encourage them to stick at things, and be persistent. The creative process doesn't always run smoothly and children get frustrated if things don't turn out as planned.

Don't worry if your child likes to spend time on his own, or in his own fantasy world. Creative children can be quite solitary – particularly if they have spent all day at school surrounded by friends and other people. It may well be that when they get home, they just want some time to themselves. I have a friend who moved house every three years or so because of work. Every time they went house-hunting, she would be on the lookout for children playing in driveways or clustered in gardens, and she would pipe through to her daughter in the back seat of the car, 'Look at that. Look at all the children to play with!' But despite her mother's best intentions, the daughter didn't want other children to play with. She preferred a couple of close friends from school, and lots of time messing around by herself. Eventually, after several house moves, my friend cottoned on to this, but not before she'd wasted a lot of hours worrying about getting her daughter lots of new friends.

But just because your child is creative doesn't mean they are condemned to long lonely evenings in their rooms. Working together with someone you trust can be the most creative thing of all. You can share ideas, and sometimes, out of that, will come new and better ideas. It's what teams of scriptwriters or designers do all the time. And it's helpful if you can show your child how this works and get them used to talking about their pet projects in an open way. They may find it scary at first to give away so much about what they're thinking and feeling, but there are plenty of ways to make it all less daunting.

Suppose your child wants to write a story, but is short of ideas. She comes to you for help. You're busy with the washing up or the end-of-month accounts, and don't have many creative juices flowing either. Or you may be tempted to give them one of your many good ideas to be getting on with. But why not try some brainstorming instead? That way your child will get used to thinking for herself, rather than using the ideas you give her, and it won't matter if you both start off slowly – with a bit of luck, you'll have got into gear by the end and found the inspiration she needs.

The idea of brainstorming is to come up with lots of suggestions. Try to 'bounce' ideas backwards and forwards, or to 'piggyback' ideas, where one person comes up with a suggestion and then the next person builds on that, adding something of their own. Don't make judgements about which ideas are good and which are bad until right at the end, when you can sift through the different things you've come up with. This way your child can give voice to ideas without worrying that someone will criticise them. And, oddly, you'll find it's easier to come up with lots of ideas than with just one, because you don't have to worry about whether the ideas are any good.

These kind of brainstorming activities show children that teamwork is one of the most creative of all activities and that they don't need to worry about sharing ideas. I've often asked children to come up with an idea for a story, only to be met by blank looks, and negative comments: 'I don't have any ideas', 'I'm not very good at stories', 'I'm not a creative person', 'Tell me what to write'. But actually, when you talk to them more closely, they have lots of ideas. What they really mean is that they don't think their ideas are any good. They think their ideas are boring. Or unoriginal. Or they're convinced that a teacher, parent or friend will think their ideas are stupid. In other words, they are either making judgements themselves about the quality of their ideas, or worrying that other people will make judgements. Every child's mind is full of memories, images, observations and dreams. It's just a question of giving children the confidence to explore their creative impulse. Brainstorming is one way of getting children to explore ideas in a supportive way, without worrying too much. It takes the pressure off. And taking the pressure off is the first step to encouraging creativity.

Finally, don't forget to tell your child he is creative. If children feel unimaginative, then they doubt themselves. Then their creativity dries up. So be positive. After all, there are few more satisfying things than seeing your child unlock their creative potential.

3. STAYING ON TOP FORM: A HEALTHY BODY AND A HEALTHY MIND

John's parents avoid giving him fizzy drinks and sugary snacks, because they believe lots of sugar has an adverse effect on his concentration. They also give him vitamin and fish-oil supplements every day, because they think it boosts his learning power. But at school, John stocks up from the tuck shop and vending machines, and always chooses chips for lunch. He doesn't believe that what he eats has any affect on his performance, although his reports suggest he's not doing as well as he could be.

Can the right diet make us smarter? Common sense tells us that it can. Food affects our mood, behaviour and concentration. And that means it can affect our ability to learn. We know that a healthy diet keeps our bodies in good shape – and the brain is part of the body. It needs water, oxygen and essential nutrients if it's to function to the best of its ability.

Sceptics point out that eating mackerel twice a week won't turn an average child into a genius. And they're right. On the other hand, a healthy diet for your child makes sense on many different levels. It's not just about better test scores. People may argue about the exact benefits of different types of food, but no one would dispute that a balanced diet makes for a healthy, happy child.

FOOD FOR LIVING

Food is the fuel of the body. More specifically, our main source of energy comes from glucose – or 'blood sugar' – which is broken down by our cells and then used for everything from getting muscles moving to powering the brain. So keeping our blood-sugar levels on an even keel is important. Too much of a surge and we feel restless. Too much of a slump and we feel listless. Neither of these is helpful to a child's learning.

One way to avoid a roller-coaster ride of highs and lows is to choose foods that release their energy slowly. These are sometimes referred to as foods with a low glycaemic index. Generally speaking, foods that contain a high proportion of refined sugar will release their energy quickly. This includes fizzy drinks, biscuits and chocolate bars. With staples like bread, pasta and rice, the processed 'white' versions release their energy more quickly than the 'brown' or wholegrain versions. These are made up of complex carbohydrates, which take longer for the body to break down. Other good slow-release foods include bananas and unsweetened cereals. And having some protein with every meal – such as meat, eggs, cheese or fish – should also help keep blood-sugar levels balanced.

Our energy levels aren't just connected to what we eat, but also to how much we eat and when. Breakfast is a must. Children often skip their morning meal because they want an extra ten minutes in bed, or because they don't feel like eating when they've just got up. With this in mind, many schools now run breakfast clubs, where pupils can have cereal, fruit and toast before lessons start. It makes breakfast more sociable and less of a rush. One study monitored the performance at school of groups of children who had either cereal for breakfast, or a glucose drink, or no breakfast at all. The groups that had the drink or no breakfast at all showed a sharp dip in concentration within an hour and a half, but the decline was much less obvious in those children who'd had the cereal.

Even with a decent breakfast, energy levels still dip naturally around mid-morning. That's why many nutritionists say it's good to graze, and that eating regularly throughout the day is the best way to stop blood-sugar levels falling. Some even argue that snacking is a human instinct, pointing out that our cave-dwelling ancestors probably just ate when they felt hungry or when food was available. The problem today is that much of the food we associate with snacks is high in salt, sugar or fat. It's not snacking itself that's unhealthy; it's the type of food children choose to snack on.

If your son tucks into a chocolate bar and washes it down with a can of fizzy pop, then his energy levels will surge. He may feel great, for a while. But the body responds to the sugar shot by producing a surge of insulin, which clears the glucose from the bloodstream. Before long he'll be back where he started, craving another hit of sugar. And when blood-sugar levels fall rapidly, the body often releases the stress hormone, adrenaline, which can make children moody and irritable.

Only the most hardline nutritionist would argue that children should never eat sweet snacks. But if a child relies on regular sugar boosts, then their energy levels are likely to fluctuate. Teachers almost always say that children are at their most difficult in the lessons between break and lunch – and they often pin the blame on the drinks and snacks that get eaten during break.

Schools that have encouraged children to cut their consumption of sugar almost always report an improvement in behaviour. Charles Burrell High School in Norfolk, for example, banned the sale of fizzy drinks on school premises, ripping out its vending machines and replaced them with water fountains. In the next few years, attendance levels improved and GCSE pass rates doubled. There were lots of reasons for the improvements, but teachers there are convinced the drinks ban played a significant part.

But getting your child to eat healthily isn't easy. Porridge? Wholewheat pasta? Lentil salad? Not dishes that are going to top many teenager wish lists. In the last five years there has been a whole raft of surveys and research looking at young people's eating habits. The findings consistently throw up alarming statistics.

Did You Know?

- Around half of children aged five to sixteen have a fizzy drink and a packet of crisps 'most days'.
- The average primary school child consumes thirty glasses of soft drinks each week.
- 45 per cent of children eat at least five more fatty foods each week than they do healthy ones.
- Between 10 and 20 per cent of four- to eighteen-year-olds eat no fruit or vegetables. Only one in nine has the recommended five portions a day.

The idea that diet can make children more intelligent or help them perform better at school is still open to dispute. The evidence is compelling, but it isn't conclusive. But what statistics like these reveal is that some children are eating so unhealthily that it's bound to have an impact on their general wellbeing. If children don't eat well, they won't feel well. And if they don't feel well, they won't learn well.

THE BATTLE AGAINST JUNK FOOD

Everyone knows that a lousy diet is bad for your waistline. But it's only recently that people have begun to wonder what impact our diet might be having on our brains. Why? Because we can see whether or not we're getting fat. We can take a look in the mirror or hop onto the scales. Other people can see it too. It's harder to monitor whether or not we're getting less clever. But that doesn't mean we should ignore the possibility that unhealthy food can affect our mental performance.

So how can you encourage your child to eat more healthily? The first step is to consider just why children – and adults – find unhealthy food appealing. It's no accident that junk food, sweets and crisps are so tempting. Manufacturers have spent many years, and millions of pounds, honing their products to make them as attractive as possible. Artificial colourings make dishes look good. Flavour enhancers add smell to food that has lost it during processing. Added salt lends even the blandest food a strong taste. Emulsifiers give products a deliciously smooth texture. And artificial sweeteners, such as aspartame or saccharin, provide a more intense sweetness than sugar can alone. Is it any wonder we're unable to resist? Then there's the convenience, the peer pressure and, of course, the hard-sell factor: almost half of all adverts aired during children's programmes promote food products.

It's hard to change eating habits overnight. And it's hard to change other habits too, like how we do things as families. Some experts, for example, advise against taking your child out for burger and chips as a treat, because it means he will associate that kind of food with happiness and good times. With your celebratory portion of fries all you are doing is reinforcing a positive image of unhealthy food. There are, of course, other options: a trip to the swimming pool, perhaps, or a game of football in the park. But most of us are more likely to see a meal out as a treat, even as adults. And would your child really choose a salad as their birthday meal of choice?

It's important not to get carried away. Eating high-fat food occasionally is unlikely to do much harm, so long as children are also eating plenty of fruit and vegetables. It's better to focus on the positives and encourage children to eat healthy food, rather than to concentrate on the negatives. Demonising some foods may only make them more attractive, especially to children who are keen to assert some independence from their parents' way of thinking. Adopt the view that there are no bad foods, only bad diets. Encourage children to eat lots of different foods. Encourage them to cook. If they learn how much butter goes into a biscuit, then they'll begin to understand why biscuits might be fattening. Encourage them to read food labels, so they can see exactly what they're eating. Don't force children to eat things they don't like, but do work hard to find things they enjoy. If they don't like apples, pears or oranges, then try pineapples, mangoes and bananas, which are sweeter, but still packed with goodness.

Did You Know?

- At Wisconsin University in the United States, researchers found that a good helping of junk food releases chemicals called opioids into the brain: the same chemicals that play a major part in drug or alcohol addiction.
- Fast food typically contains 65 per cent more calories per bite than an average British meal. Which means a child tucking into a cheap hamburger and fries will consume many more calories than a child eating the same weight of pasta and salad.
- The food industry's global advertising budget is $40 billion, more than the gross domestic product of 70 per cent of the world's nations.

The key to cutting out the junk food seems to lie in educating children about why diet matters so they can see it's about more than grumpy parents ganging up against chips. If children understand how food works in their bodies and why some foods are better for them than others, then they'll be able to make informed choices. Since the government started its drive to make school lunches more healthy, and to teach children more about nutrition issues, there are signs that things are improving. High-fat foods and chips still make up 20 per cent of the food eaten in primary schools, but fruit, vegetables and salads now make up an almost identical proportion. Most children don't want to be fat. They want to be full of life and energy. They want to feel healthy. But if they're accustomed to a diet of high-fat, flavour-enhanced food, it's understandable if some other foods seem to lack punch.

Little by little it's possible to change eating habits. And once children start to enjoy healthy foods, they'll automatically start to cut down on the unhealthy ones. If they get used to food that's unseasoned, then perhaps that bag of crisps will seem just too salty. If they get a taste for grilled chicken breast, then maybe those nuggets won't be so appealing. If they learn to love apple juice, then they could well cut down on the cola. If your child still seems to prefer burgers and crisps to anything else, it may be worth giving them a zinc supplement. Zinc deficiency reduces the ability to taste and smell and so prompts cravings for very sweet, salty or spicy foods.

WATER

A lack of water can make children feel tired and sluggish. One study showed that drinking a glass of water when thirsty improved mental performance by 10 per cent. It's always best to be wary of these kind of headline-grabbing statistics but in this case there's plenty of anecdotal evidence to back up the research. In schools where children have been encouraged to drink more water, teachers are convinced that it has made a difference. At Dihewyd Primary School in Wales, every child has their own water bottle, which they refill regularly and keep on their desk throughout the day. Teachers claim pupils are calmer and more focused on their work and that concentration levels are higher, particularly towards the end of the day. The children agree, with most of them saying they have more energy and feel more awake.

So why does water make us feel more alert? After all, it contains no 'energy' as such. Scientists don't have a perfect understanding, but water seems to play an important role in conducting electrical impulses to and around the brain. Being well hydrated may also allow our red blood cells to carry more oxygen to the brain, which improves our mental abilities.

But it's not necessarily a case of the more, the better. Studies have also shown that drinking more water than we need, or drinking very cold water, can actually cause a temporary dip in our mental abilities as the body diverts energy into rebalancing its hydration levels. Nor is anyone quite sure just how much water is the right amount. Some guidelines suggest three or four glasses a day, while others advise twice that amount. The reality is that the amount of water we need to drink varies from person to person, and from day to day. If your child has a sweaty PE lesson or plays football during break, they'll need more water than if they're just sat in the classroom. And sitting in a hot, stuffy classroom will be more dehydrating than being in a cool, well-ventilated one. Stressful situations can also cause sweating and dehydration, so children may need to drink more water around exam time, or on the day of a big test.

The key is not to wait for hours and then gulp down litres at a time. The body can only absorb water relatively slowly, so sipping regularly throughout the day is the best way to stay properly hydrated. And it's about a bit of variety. If your child doesn't like water, or if they fancy a change, then weak cordials or squashes are fine. A small amount of fruit juice, diluted with sparkling water, is another possibility. Fizzy pop drinks can be hydrating, but if you got all your water from them, you'd also be getting far too much sugar!

If we don't drink enough water it can lead to mild

dehydration, which causes headaches and a general feeling of tiredness. But many children – and adults – have grown used to feeling slightly below par, so they don't recognise the warning signs. Telling children that they should take a drink whenever they feel thirsty seems like sound advice, but often we only start to feel thirsty after the effects of dehydration have begun to set in. If you think your child may not be getting enough to drink then the best thing is to get him to check the colour of his urine. It should be pale: if it's dark yellow then he's dehydrated.

Since we're lucky enough to have free, fresh and relatively decent water on tap, why might children not drink enough water during the day? At home, there's really no excuse. But at school, it's more complicated. I've spoken to some children who say they don't drink any water at all during the school day. Some said they didn't like drinking from taps or old-fashioned water fountains, where they had to lean over and slurp water into their mouth. They didn't think it was hygienic, or they worried that someone would push them and they'd bump their teeth. One child was concerned that if he drank lots of water, he might have to ask to go to the toilet during a lesson, which his teacher didn't like. Another said the school water tasted nasty. She was right. Another pointed out that he was not allowed to drink during lessons, so could only get water during break or lunch when everyone else was trying to get a drink at the same time. Another said she could only get water from the taps in the toilets, and she didn't like going there because that's where the school bullies hung out. To the children concerned, these were all good reasons for not drinking water.

Fortunately, things are improving. Many schools now allow children to drink water during lessons. Others have installed water coolers in the corridors, linked to the mains, so it's easy for children to grab a drink as they're passing. The reality is that most children probably do drink enough water, but it's still worth keeping an eye out for signs of dehydration. If your child complains of finding it difficult to concentrate, or of feeling tired in the afternoons, then it may be that an extra glass or two of water will make a difference. And talk to them, too, about their habits at school. It may show you that it's not a question of them forgetting to drink, or of not wanting to, but that the simple task of getting a glass of water is mixed up with all kinds of other concerns about getting through the school day.

Things To Do

- Most of us don't actually know how much water we drink over the course of an average day. The only way to find out is to get your child to keep a record for a day or two. See how that measures up against suggested guidelines.
- Don't be too alarmed if your child seems to drink very little water. Lots of other drinks contain water, so they help to hydrate the body, even if they're not as beneficial as plain water. And there's water in food too, especially in fruits, vegetables and salads.
- Encourage your child to try drinking more water, for a trial period of one week. Ask them if they notice any improvements or feel more alert.
- Give your child a bottle of water to take to school. It doesn't have to be filled with mineral water. Most studies show that tap water is clean, and just as healthy.

OMEGA-3: THE KEY TO A BETTER BRAIN?

Eating well makes children healthy and happy. It gives them the energy and enthusiasm to cope with a demanding day in school. It helps their concentration. It makes them better learners. But do certain foods actually make children more clever? Can diet directly affect intelligence?

The search for a 'brain pill' that can boost intelligence has led scientists in the direction of omega-3. That's the name of a group of 'fatty acids', which are present in the brain, and which seem to play a crucial role in the smooth running of our thought processes. Omega-3 is found in oily fish, such as sardines and mackerel. So the old saying that fish is good for the brain probably isn't far wide of the mark.

The bad news is that oily fish isn't popular with children. Given the choice between a pizza or a piece of smoked mackerel, not many kids are going to plump for the fish. Other foods have fatty acids in them, like walnuts and pumpkin seeds, but not to the same extent. Fatty acids are hardly ever found in processed foods, and one report suggests that there has been an 80 per cent decline in the intake of fatty acids over the last century. The good news is that fish-oil tablets are widely available as a dietary supplement. But they're not cheap. So where's the evidence that they're worth spending money on?

At first glance, results from trials in which children have been given a daily supplement of fish oil seem fairly convincing:

- At Newhall Park Primary School in Bradford, over two-thirds of the children who were given fish oils showed improvement in literacy and numeracy.
- The head teacher at Newton Aycliffe Secondary School in Durham claims that giving omega-3 supplements three times a day to a group of children with learning difficulties had 'a significant impact'.
- The so-called Oxford–Durham project, headed by Professor Alex Richardson of Oxford University, gave supplements to a group of children aged five to twelve. The children were all judged to be slightly below average in terms of their results, but not in terms of ability. Many of them had dysphasia, a motor-neurone problem that can cause children to have difficulties with their co-ordination. Those children who were given supplements containing omega-3, omega-6 and

vitamin E made nine months' progress with their reading in the three months they took the supplements. The control group, who were given capsules containing olive oil, made the expected three months' progress. When the control group were later given the supplements, they began to make similar progress. There was also some evidence that short-term memory improved.

- Research carried out at the University of Bristol found that the children of mothers who eat plenty of fish have better communication and social skills. The researchers looked at the IQ and communication skills of children aged up to eight years old, and quizzed their mothers about their fish consumption. The study found that eating little or no fish was associated with a 48 per cent increased risk of children being in the lowest group for verbal intelligence.

- As well as boosting academic performance, research suggests that omega-3 can help to reduce aggressive behaviour. A trial at Aylesbury Prison found that when inmates were given supplements, incidents of violent behaviour fell by 37 per cent. Meanwhile, other studies have suggested omega-3 may play a part in preventing depression.

So what do all those findings add up to? Should you be rushing down to the chemist or the fishmonger?

Well, despite the impressive statistics above, the research to date is by no means conclusive. Far from it. The study in Bradford, for example, was sponsored by Boots, and wasn't scientifically rigorous. The most reliable of the trials is probably the Oxford–Durham study, but this was specific to pupils with learning difficulties, and didn't look at the effect of fish oils on ordinary children. The evidence has not been enough to convince the government who, for a time, were considering a national programme of fish-oil supplements, before deciding that the studies just weren't compelling enough.

And yet . . . the links between omega-3 and brain function

won't go away. In the great scheme of things, research is still at an early stage. The next five years are likely to bring new findings and new evidence. And the eyewitness accounts given by teachers and head teachers in the schools involved in trials suggest they have seen real differences in pupils given the supplements, even if the statistics and the research methods were sometimes flawed.

And while there is doubt about the exact benefits of omega-3, there are currently no concerns about possible adverse effects. So perhaps it's not much of a gamble. If omega-3 does boost brainpower, then great. If it doesn't, so what? Other than your hard-earned cash, what do you have to lose?

Scientists aren't quite sure why omega-3 might be important. Some say it helps to improve blood flow. More interesting, though, is the idea that omega-3 plays an important part in our thought processes. Electrical signals in the brain get passed from one brain cell to the next through cell membranes that consist largely of fat. And a proportion of that fat is omega-3. One theory is that omega-3 makes it easier for signals to pass from one cell to the next, possibly by making the cell membranes more flexible, so the brain works more efficiently. There are two omega-3 fatty acids – DHA and EPA – that seem more important than the others. The theory is that a deficiency of these acids means our brain cells form fewer connections with other brain cells, and don't pass on information as quickly.

Omega-3 fatty acids seem to play a particularly important part in the transmission of signals relating to our vision. That may possibly explain why omega-3 deficiency has been linked to conditions such as dyslexia, where children sometimes say that the letters jump around in front of their eyes, and dysphasia, where children may be clumsy or unco-ordinated. Some scientists believe that a ready supply of omega-3 oils is particularly important in the developing foetus, and that without it our brain will be less flexible and efficient. It's also thought that less healthy fats, known as trans fats, found in some fast foods, are instinctively used by the body in the same way as omega-3, but with dire consequences. Because these fats are thought to be very poor at conducting impulses they have the exact opposite effect and 'clog up' the brain.

If you're not convinced about the benefits of omega-3, or don't like the idea of giving your child supplements, then at least try to put fish on the menu once or twice a week. Many nutritionists say that getting our omega-3 from food is better than getting it from pills, because we're also getting some of the minerals that help the body to make good use of the oil. Fresh tuna is a good source of omega-3. From time to time there are concerns about mercury levels in some kinds of tuna, but experts say the health benefits far outweigh any possible risks. Salmon and trout are also both rich in omega-3, while sardines, mackerel and herring have the advantage of being cheap. And even white fish, like cod or haddock, contain a small amount of omega-3, as do most nuts and seeds, and some vegetables, including spinach. Given that many omega-3 supplements work out at between 50p and £1 a day, if you were to spend that money on adding some healthy extras to the shopping basket, it would go a long way. Good overall nutrition is still more important than one single element, and there's probably not much benefit to your child taking supplements if the rest of the time they're munching on burgers and biscuits.

Next Steps

If you and your child do decide to try some fish-oil supplements, you'll probably find yourselves faced with a bewildering selection. The omega-3 industry is big business, so much so that concerns have been raised about its impact on future fish stocks. In 2003, following a wave of publicity about omega-3, sales of supplements more than quadrupled.

Prices vary, but to get a real idea of cost you need to

look at the amount of omega-3 contained in each tablet or capsule. A daily dose of 500mg is the usual recommendation, so work out how many tablets will be needed to deliver that quantity of omega-3. Some tablets also contain omega-6 oils, which are thought to be beneficial. And some contain added vitamins too, though that may mean you have to be extra careful not to exceed the stated dose.

You can buy capsules, tablets, liquids or powders. For younger children a liquid supplement may be easiest, while older ones will probably prefer capsules they can carry around easily in their pockets. Products also vary widely in taste, so you may need to experiment with different brands before finding one your child likes. Some capsules contain artificial sweeteners and colourings, which you may want to avoid.

Finally, be aware that traditional cod-liver oil isn't a substitute for specialist supplements. It's not particularly rich in the important omega-3 oils, like DHA.

For more information about the research into omega-3 visit www.fabresearch.org, the website of Food and Behaviour Research, a charitable organisation that publishes the latest research on links between nutrition and human behaviour.

CARING FOR THE BRAIN

The brain is greedy. It makes up only around 2 per cent of our weight, but uses around 20 per cent of our body's energy and around a quarter of the blood from the heart. It's also a bit of a picky eater. It needs specific nutrients to function at its peak. The B-group of vitamins are thought to be particularly important. They tend to occur in wholegrain cereals, and in vegetables, fruit, meat and poultry. So anyone with a reasonably balanced diet should be fine. Because the brain works through a series of nerve impulses, minerals that play an important role in nerve activity are probably also important. These include magnesium, which is found in green vegetables and nuts, and potassium, which is found in bananas, strawberries and kiwi fruit.

But it's probably not worth worrying specifically about the brain's requirements. Better by far just to feed your child a healthy balanced diet. Almost all fruit and vegetables offer some valuable minerals and vitamins. If you can get your child eating something approaching the government's recommended target of five portions a day then chances are he'll be getting all the right nutrients for his brain, especially if those five portions contain plenty of variety. Bananas are probably the most popular fruit among younger children and, luckily, they're also one of the healthiest.

As well as nutrients, the brain needs oxygen. That's why exercise is important: it improves blood circulation, and it's the blood that carries oxygen to the brain and takes away waste materials. A study at Mellor Primary School in Leicester found that children who were placed in a special 'exercise group' for 9 months made a gain of 23 months in reading compared to a gain of 12 months in the control group. In itself that doesn't prove anything, but it certainly fits with the idea that exercise is good for the brain. And once we start thinking of the brain as a part of the body, an organ, like the heart or the lungs, it becomes logical to think that exercise will be beneficial. Even a half-hour walk each day is likely to make children feel healthier physically and sharper mentally. In fact, walking may be especially good for the brain, since it promotes blood flow, but isn't too strenuous, so the body's resources aren't diverted to other areas, like the leg muscles. There's even some evidence that exercise can help promote new growth of brain cells, and trials with elderly people have shown that regular exercise leads to a better memory. There seems to be no good reason why the same shouldn't also be true for younger people. But even when we're just watching TV or doing homework, the way we breathe can affect the amount of oxygen that gets to the brain. Deep, regular breathing is best. If we breathe too rapidly, then our blood vessels may narrow and less oxygen will be released from the blood into our cells.

Finally, there's one more thing the brain needs, and that's rest. Scientists have found that after a long time without sleep most people's IQ scores drop sharply. So do their concentration levels. But after a good night's sleep they'll be back to their normal level. Not that the brain just shuts down during sleep. Most people have probably had the experience of going to bed unable to remember something, or unable to solve a puzzle, only to wake up and find their brain has been doing some useful work during the night. And we all dream, of course. In fact some experts think certain parts of the brain are actually busier at night. It may be that this is the time when our brain orders the information processed during the day. Some studies suggest that during sleep the brain transfers things from short-term to long-term memory. In particular, sleep seems to help our brains secure what are called 'procedural memories' – so if you're learning a dance routine or how to juggle, you may find that you wake up one morning and it's all clicked into place. One study got participants to remember and type out a sequence on a keyboard. After a night's sleep, they performed 20 per cent better.

Whatever happens during sleep, one thing's for sure – without it our brains start to suffer. I've watched some lessons in school where a significant number of the children in the class have clearly been tired. When I chatted to one boy who'd spent the lesson with his head on the desk, he told me that he'd been up since five in the morning every day that week, helping sort the papers in a newsagent's. It wasn't hard to see that if he did that every day, week in, week out, his results in school were going to take a hit. Whether it's early-morning paper rounds or late-night films, anything that stops children getting enough sleep can cause problems.

But how much sleep is enough? For most children eight

hours a night is probably a reliable guide – but younger children may need considerably more. Of course, you can't force your child to go to sleep, but you should certainly keep an eye out for signs of tiredness. I was never sure whether the parents of that boy who got up at five each morning ever knew how tired he was at school. Perhaps after spending all day with his head on the desk, he went home each evening looking wide awake! They probably also didn't realise they were breaking the law. School-aged children aren't allowed to do paid work before seven in the morning, or to work for more than two hours on a school day.

Whatever the reasons, an occasional late night or early morning won't do any harm. But long-term tiredness will certainly stop children performing at their best.

Things To Do

There's nothing here that isn't plain common sense. Even so, it's worth saying it all over again:

- Try to give your child meals that release their energy slowly. That means choosing complex carbohydrates, and avoiding too many refined sugars.
- Breakfast is important. Scrambled eggs on toast are good. So is porridge, and perhaps some fruit or nuts.
- Encourage your child to drink plenty of plain water, at least four or five glasses a day.
- Make sure they get a good night's sleep, especially before a school day.
- Try to get them to eat oily fish once or twice each week. If they won't, then consider an omega-3 supplement.
- Aim for five portions of fruit or vegetables every day. If that proves tricky then, again, consider a supplement.
- Encourage your child to do at least twenty minutes' exercise every day, even if it's just a walk.

4. UNDERSTANDING EMOTIONAL INTELLIGENCE: WHAT IT IS AND WHY IT MATTERS

Emma used to do well at school. She learned quickly and she could read and write above the level expected of her age group. But recently she seems to have lost motivation. She doesn't care about her lessons, and she's fallen out with her friends. She's becoming sulky. And her work is suffering; her grades are falling, and her teachers are complaining. Things seem to be getting on top of her, and she's struggling to find a way to cope.

Success at school, and in life, is not just dependent on academic skills and IQ. The more a child is able to identify, understand and manage her emotions, the more likely she is to come out on top. The more understanding she has of other people's feelings, too, the more she is likely to be happy and settled.

THE BASICS OF EMOTIONAL INTELLIGENCE

There are lots of definitions of emotional intelligence. Most of them are long-winded and unhelpful. So let's keep it simple. Instead of trying to define what emotional intelligence is, let's look at how it reveals itself. In other words, what are the qualities of an emotionally intelligent person?

An emotionally intelligent person is able to understand the emotions they are feeling. Sounds simple, doesn't it? But emotions can be complex things and it's perfectly possible to feel varied or conflicting emotions at the same time, such as fear and excitement, or anger and sadness. The emotionally intelligent person is able to analyse the exact nature of *what* they are feeling. More importantly, they are also able to understand *why* they are feeling that way. They can think about the circumstances that cause them to feel the way they do. Finally – and most importantly of all – the emotionally intelligent person is able to learn from their feelings. When faced with negative emotions, they don't repress them, or lash out in frustration. Instead they turn them into positive learning experiences. They are able to change their behaviour, and work out *how* they can avoid these negative emotions in the future.

Our lives are a cycle of emotions, thoughts and actions. The way we think affects the way we feel, the way we feel affects the way we act, the way we act can change the way we feel. And so it goes on. The emotionally intelligent person is able to control this cycle, rather than be controlled by it.

Did You Know?

- The term emotional intelligence became widely known in 1995, when Daniel Goleman, a US psychologist and science writer, published the bestselling book *Emotional Intelligence – Why It Can Matter More Than IQ*. It sold more than five million copies worldwide.

- The book claimed that IQ only accounted for 20 per cent of people's success and that in many situations emotional intelligence was much more important. As a result, many companies and businesses bought into the idea of training their workforce to be more emotionally intelligent.
- Goleman's book drew on the research of academics John Mayer and Peter Salovey. They have since been critical of Goleman's approach to the subject.

Emotional intelligence isn't just about you. It's also about other people. An emotionally intelligent person has the ability to understand how other people are feeling. They are sensitive to body language, facial expression and tone of voice. They can understand how their own actions affect others. And they are able to help friends by sharing in their feelings, or offering good advice in times of need.

EMOTIONAL INTELLIGENCE AT SCHOOL

The word 'intelligence' can be misleading. Emotional Intelligence is not the same thing as cognitive intelligence, the thinking that helps us work out maths sums or put together an essay. Brilliant academics don't always have great people skills. But there's no doubt that having a high level of emotional intelligence can help young people to achieve at school and beyond.

I've known many children who have been de-motivated or disinterested at school. And very often it's because they feel alienated. They don't fit into the social network. They don't get on with the people in their class, or with their teachers. They feel lonely or victimised. In that kind of situation it can be almost impossible for a child to focus successfully on their studies. Children who are emotionally intelligent, on the other hand, are likely to have high self-esteem, a strong network of friends, and good relationships with their teachers. All of which means that they are likely to have a positive attitude to school. And children with a positive attitude to school tend to perform well and fulfil their potential.

A high level of emotional intelligence helps young people to stay motivated when they are faced with things they don't want to do. Children often take a short-term view when it comes to school. It's more fun to talk to friends than to listen to the teacher. Playing football in the park is more appealing than the geography coursework that's due in next week. But a child with a higher level of emotional intelligence is more likely to see the bigger picture. If they work hard, they will get good grades, go on to university, get a good job, and spend many happy years doing what they most want to do.

Many schools now teach some kind of emotional intelligence course. There's all kinds of different names for these: emotional awareness, perhaps, or emotional literacy (which emphasises the ways we *read* our own or other people's feelings). But whatever the title, the basics are the same: encouraging pupils to speak about their emotions and trying to make them more aware of how others are feeling. Schools that introduce this kind of programme say that behaviour in lessons improves beyond recognition. After all, disruptive actions in the classroom are nearly always the result of children not being able to handle their own emotions, or not taking other people's feelings into consideration. That's why children bully, shout out, or distract others. When children who struggle to understand the work try to disrupt others, it's because they can't handle the feelings of frustration they experience. The more emotionally intelligent a child is, the more likely they are to curb their impulsive behaviour.

Success at school isn't just a question of cognitive intelligence. It's a question of emotional intelligence too. And the child that manages to combine a high IQ with a high EQ is likely to be successful at school, and at work, and in their personal life.

Did You Know?

- Way back in 1997, schools in Southampton began teaching a programme of emotional literacy, and in 2005 the Department for Education and Skills sent out material to all primary schools, encouraging them to teach five key emotional skills – self-awareness, managing emotions, empathy, communication and motivation.
- In the same way as IQ tests measure intellectual intelligence, there are now many tests that claim to measure EQ, or emotional quotient. But many people have questioned the reliability of these tests, as they can't replicate the real-life situations and relationships in which our emotions are tested.
- Research at Case Western Reserve University in Ohio has shown that children who experience feelings of rejection see their IQ scores fall by up to 25 per cent.

DEVELOPING EMOTIONAL INTELLIGENCE

Emotional intelligence is something we are all born with. As babies, we experience a range of emotions, like fear or happiness. And we are able to communicate those emotions to other people, by crying or laughing. As with other kinds of intelligence, some children seem more naturally gifted than others. They communicate their feelings openly and easily, and seem quick to pick up on any anxiety or anger displayed by those around them.

But it's possible to nurture children's innate abilities – to turn their emotional intelligence into a practical set of skills that will help them in life. Just as we can teach children to read and write, so we can teach them to be emotionally literate.

Things To Do

- Most films, as well as soaps and dramas on television, centre around emotions. Talk to your child about how characters in a programme might be feeling, why they might feel that way, and how they are showing their feelings.
- Reading books is a great way of improving emotional intelligence, because young people learn to relate to the characters, and to put themselves into other people's shoes. Drama is even better because they can play at being other people. If there's a drama club at your child's school, encourage them to join.
- With younger children, looking at photographs in magazines or books can be helpful. Get them to look at the expression on people's faces, to try to work out what they might be feeling.

Try to encourage all the members of your family to express their emotions and to feel comfortable with the effects of strong feelings. If a child displays negative emotions such as sadness or anger, most parents' first reaction is to tell them to cheer up or calm down. But this can give the impression that these feelings are 'wrong'. It's more important to find out why they're feeling sad or angry. To get them to talk about their feelings and encourage them to recognise and value their emotions. Telling children to put on a happy face when they're feeling sad is unlikely to do much to raise their emotional intelligence.

But it's hard. Society demands that grown-ups hide their emotions much of the time. Adults don't go around shouting every time they get angry, or crying in public. Children have the freedom to be more expressive, but only to a degree. The important thing is to help your child understand the difference between feelings and actions. So it's acceptable to feel angry, but not acceptable to lash out or hit someone.

The more able your child is to talk about her emotions, the more likely she is to be able to control her actions. So try to encourage her to talk to you about how she's feeling, even when it all seems very ordinary. Sometimes we only take an interest if there's a display of a strong emotion like sadness or joy. Getting children to talk about their day-to-day feelings will make it easier for them to open up when they are trying to cope with more intense emotions.

Young people often struggle to express their feelings accurately in words. Some will hide their emotions. It may be obvious that something's wrong, but they just shrug and say, 'I'm fine'. It could be that they feel talking about what's bothering them will upset you, or that you might disapprove of the way they are feeling. It could be that they think – rightly or wrongly – that you won't take any notice of what they say. Or it may be that they simply lack the vocabulary to express how they are feeling. They can't put it into words.

If that's the case, you might have to encourage your child to talk around her emotions, prompting along the way, offering some words that might be helpful.

Offering some kind of structure might help your child express herself. With younger children it's often useful to use a scale of 1 to 10, to indicate the strength of their feeling. This can be especially helpful with children who tend to exaggerate how they're feeling. Children who overplay their emotions often do it because they feel it's the only way they'll get attention. Getting them to think about a scale, and talking as much about feelings that register down at number one or two as about those that hit nine or ten, should help them see that they don't have to be making a fuss to have something valid to say about the way they're feeling. As children grow older, work on expanding their emotional vocabulary, so they can be more specific about their emotions. Showing that you are happy to listen, whatever your child is feeling, is the best way of encouraging her to be accurate and honest.

Things To Do

- Explain to your child how our feelings can be an important factor when we're making decisions. Encourage them to think through the emotional consequences of their actions. 'If I do this, how will Mum feel? How will Dad feel? How will I feel?'

- To develop emotional intelligence, it's important to remember the emotions we experience. Keeping a diary that focuses on feelings can be a helpful way of doing that. If your child remembers what it feels like to be sad, then they will have more understanding when a friend is in the same position.

- Encourage your child to express their feelings. A child who is annoyed with a friend will often say something like, 'Jake is stupid', or 'Jake makes me angry'. However, it may be more helpful if they are able to say, 'I am angry with Jake because . . .'

- Don't forget to praise your child when they show good emotional skills, just as you might praise them if they did well in academic work. If they say something nice to a friend, for example, you could take time later to just say, 'That was a nice thing you did there . . .'

- As children get older, help them to expand their vocabulary of 'feeling' words. This list is just for starters: unhappy, accepted, rejected, abandoned, left out, criticised, lectured to, preached to, mocked, appreciated, unappreciated, supported, unsupported, uncomfortable, optimistic, pessimistic, hopeful, hopeless, discouraged, encouraged, afraid, motivated, unmotivated, free, controlled, bored, guilty, embarrassed, ashamed, in control, out of control, jealous, sad, lonely, ignored, important, unimportant, proud, confident, worthy, happy, loved, excited, fulfilled, angry, frustrated.

As always, it's important to set a good example with the way that you handle your own emotions. You have to communicate clearly. Talk to your child about how you are feeling. Don't be afraid of saying when you're sad. In particular, let her know how her actions and behaviour make you feel. And remember, all children are emotionally intelligent to a greater or lesser degree. That means they can read your non-verbal language. If your mouth is saying one thing, but your face and body are saying another, then your child will pick up on it. They'll be confused. Or they'll know that you're being dishonest. If you want to encourage emotional intelligence it's best to say what you mean, and mean what you say. You have to be a good emotional role model.

Next Steps

Antidote is an organisation that promotes the teaching of emotional literacy in schools and other organisations. To find out more about what they are doing, you can visit their website (www.antidote.org).

Part II

SMART SCHOOLING

5. MAKING THE RIGHT CHOICE: CHOOSING A GOOD SCHOOL AND GETTING YOUR CHILD ACCEPTED

Ben's parents are moving house. They are crossing the country to an area they don't know. They need to find Ben a new school. They need to find Ben a good school. He's a boy with a lot of potential, and they want somewhere that will work with them to inspire and stimulate him. But where do they start?

Here are a few figures: the UK has the highest rates of truancy and exclusion in Europe. Over 16,000 primary school children are taught in classes of more than thirty pupils. Only around half of all sixteen-year-olds manage five GCSEs at grade C or above. And each year, Ofsted reports that around 1,500 schools perform badly.

There are some awful schools out there. Schools that some children are stuck in day after day, week after week, year after year. But there are some excellent schools too. It's just a question of finding one – and then getting your child a place there.

REPUTATIONS

The chances are you already have an opinion about the best schools in your area. But what is it based on? Exam grades? Sports results? Gossip? All schools have reputations, good or bad. But it's not always clear where they come from. Good behaviour at the bus stops may have more to do with it than the excellence of teaching. And be warned: schools change quickly, local opinions don't. The reputation of a school is probably an accurate reflection of what it was like five years ago. Perhaps things have changed, perhaps they haven't. It's up to you to find out.

If you're deciding which school to send your child to, then you'll want to do some research. Talking to parents who already have children there is a good first step. Having a look at the school's prospectus is another obvious idea. All schools are legally bound to publish one of these, and they give you a basic picture of what the school is about. Nowadays they're often produced as a DVD, so you can skip through the boring bits! Most schools also have a website, and this is usually much more informative and up to date than the prospectus. Because it's aimed at current parents and pupils, not just potential ones, it's often more honest and revealing. Try having a good look through the section marked 'calendar' or 'events': it should give you a real flavour of just how much is going on from day to day.

But remember that a prospectus or a website is essentially a marketing tool. Head teachers are pretty media-savvy these days. They have sizeable marketing budgets and employ public relations consultants to help get good coverage in the local papers. So don't be taken in by the glossy brochures and the press cuttings. You need to see through the marketing and make your mind up for yourself.

LEAGUE TABLES

Information about schools is more freely available than ever before. You just need to make sense of it. The government denies that it publishes league tables – and in a sense that's true. It publishes information about how a school has performed, based on SATs scores and exams results. It's usually local newspapers that then use that information to produce a 'league table', showing how schools have done in comparison to their neighbours.

But whatever the subtleties of the system, the fact is there *will* be a league table that includes all your local schools. You *will* be able to see who's coming out on top, and who's marooned in the relegation zone. The question is, will it really make you any the wiser? Is it a good way of choosing a school?

Some people think league tables can only be a good thing. If a school is near the bottom, then it will be forced to pull its socks up, so standards will improve. And if a school is doing badly, then parents have a right to know, so they can choose a different school; one that's getting better results. These are both sound arguments in favour of league tables.

But critics argue that education is too complex to be reduced to a simple set of percentages. They argue that tables only reflect a school's academic performance, and don't tell you anything about the pastoral care it offers, or its extra-curricular activities. And schools that perform badly in the tables can find it difficult to attract new teachers, while existing staff are more likely to become de-motivated. A 2005 survey by the Teacher Support Network found that 70 per cent of primary teachers felt league tables had a negative effect on their wellbeing.

But perhaps the biggest argument against league tables is that they don't tell you very much about the quality of teaching in a school. Schools that come out best are usually those that serve prosperous middle-class suburbs. Critics argue that league tables don't tell you how good a school is, they just tell you how wealthy the parents are.

Whichever side of the fence you fall, it's unlikely you'll be able to resist taking a quick look at the local league. Just a peek. Just out of interest. So it's important to know what you're looking at. There's more to a league table than just the bare results. And the more sense you can make from the information, the more helpful it's likely to be.

When it comes to checking out the statistics, you'll be faced with two sets of figures. The first tells you how many children reached the expected level for their age group, in SATs, GCSEs or A levels. This might seem straightforward, but of course it's not. Sometimes the statistics can be plain misleading, so be wary. For example, one of the figures often used in league tables is based on the number of children at the school who get five GCSEs at grades A–C. Let's imagine a school where a hundred pupils get five passes, all at grade C. Result – 100 per cent. Let's imagine another school where ninety pupils get eight passes at grade A, but ten pupils only get four passes at grade C. Result – a 90 per cent pass rate, well below the other school. But which one got the best results? It's not straightforward.

And statistics don't always give you the full picture. They might tell you that one school is doing better than another, but they don't give you any insight into why that's happening. Nor do they take account of particular circumstances. In small schools, for example, results can fluctuate wildly from year to year: it might only take a couple of pupils to do exceptionally well or badly to make a drastic difference to the figures.

The second set of figures in the table is the 'value added' scores. These are calculated by comparing pupils' results against their past performances to see if they've made more or less progress than might be expected. In theory, that should give you a better indication of the quality of teaching in a school than just a list of results. But in practice, schools that do well in the basic results table also do well in the value-added tables. Which is no help at all.

So now the government is phasing in a new set of figures called CVA, which stands for Contextual Value Added. This means the figures are adjusted to take account of factors such as the number of children at the school who are from disadvantaged backgrounds. The CVA should give some useful information about how well schools are doing within their own particular constraints, but it also makes things even more complicated.

Value-added figures may be useful for head teachers and school governors, but most parents are only interested in the bottom line. Good results. After all, in the real world, it's real results that count. Is any parent seriously going to choose a school that gets moderate results, but where children make good progress, over one where children make slower progress but get excellent results? Comparing schools is very difficult. Like the children they serve, every school is unique. Perhaps it's not surprising that fewer than one in three parents say they take any notice of league tables.

INSPECTION REPORTS

In principle, an inspection report should be an excellent guide when you're looking to choose a school. In England inspections are carried out by Ofsted, and there are similar inspection bodies in Wales (Estyn) and Scotland (HMIE). Schools will give you a copy of their latest inspection report on request. And all reports are available online, which makes it easy to compare the reports of different schools in your area. In theory, an inspection report should tell you much more than the league table statistics. Inspectors watch teachers in action and talk to pupils about their work, which is definitely a good thing. Reports give a summary of the overall performance of the school and the quality of the school's leadership and management. There's a detailed breakdown of how well each subject is taught, with different departments rated as outstanding, very good, good, satisfactory or unsatisfactory. There's also a section highlighting areas where the inspectors feel the school needs to improve.

> ### Did You Know?
> - The average child spends around 17,000 hours in school.
> - A million children are in schools that Ofsted labels 'poorly performing'.
> - The gap between the best and worst comprehensives is widening.

But most teachers, head teachers and education experts have reservations about the quality and reliability of school inspections, particularly in England. There's a lack of consistency, which makes it hard to compare different schools. Some inspection teams are excellent and fair-minded, while others set out to find fault, and tend to overlook the positives. Ofsted argues that inspectors work to set criteria, and that the personality and prejudices of inspectors don't come into it. But that's not the view of most head teachers.

Another problem with reports is that very often, instead of telling you more than the league tables, they just tell you the same thing. That's because the test scores and exam statistics are the first things the inspectors look at – even before they've been to the school. These statistics are the single biggest factor in influencing the report. But school results vary from year to year, and aren't always a direct reflection of the quality of teaching and learning. Another thing to bear in mind is that Ofsted is a government department. It is fond of head teachers who can recite the latest government initiatives by heart. It likes schools that do as they are told. But some of the best schools break the mould, and some of the best head teachers have a distinctive vision.

I've seen many cases where a school's inspection report hasn't told the full picture. I once visited a primary school near Cannock, in Staffordshire. The school was fantastic. Children were encouraged to be creative. There were free music lessons for every child. There was some very impressive project work in art and science. And the children were interested in the learning process, and keen to talk about their work. But the school was situated in a former mining town, and its results were typical of schools in similar catchment areas, with standards of literacy and numeracy slightly below the average. Rather than focus on what the children couldn't do, the head teacher focused on the positives. She knew that if the children were enjoying school, their confidence would grow, and improvements in literacy and numeracy would follow. The inspectors didn't agree. They said the school should make reading and writing a part of every lesson, in order to raise standards. The head refused. She argued that forcing children to do lots of writing, lesson after lesson, would just make them less enthusiastic. They would lose confidence, then lose interest. The inspectors pointed to disappointing SATs results the previous year. The head explained that it was a difficult year group, and that the current year's results, published in just a few months' time, would be much better. The inspectors placed the school in special measures and the head resigned. The new results came out, and the school was among the most improved hundred schools in the country. Its results were well above the average for its catchment area. The head's philosophy had been vindicated.

That's just one of many examples I could give. The reality is that inspection reports and exam statistics can only ever tell part of the story. And if they are more than twelve months old, then they may well be out of date. Things change quickly, especially if a new head moves in. So treat reports with caution. By far the best way of judging a school is to pay it a visit.

VISITING A SCHOOL

You're not just looking for a good school – you're looking for the right school for *your* child. Don't rely on facts and figures, or local gossip, or cobbled-together reports. Trust your own eyes and ears. Meet the head. Ask questions. Take a tour of the school, preferably given by one of the older pupils. Ask more questions.

A good school is one where children go about their learning in a happy, relaxed and co-operative atmosphere. You can usually identify this kind of productive environment – or the lack of it – within minutes of walking through the gates. And remember that your child's progress will be largely determined by his attitude to school. So listen to what he has to say. His opinion matters just as much as yours, and on a tour of the school he'll pick up on different things to you. Swap notes and share impressions. If you send him to a school he's not keen on, for whatever reason, then he may struggle to settle.

Lots of schools hold open days, where they invite local parents to come and have a look round. These are a good idea, but you need to remember that you'll be seeing the school at its very best. Visit in the week prior to an open day, and you may well find displays being made, walls being painted, bookshelves tidied and activities frantically rehearsed. By the time the day dawns, litter will be swept away, floors polished, windows cleaned and flowerbeds weeded. There will be hired plants in the corridors, pristine sports kit on the playing fields and the best china by the tea urn.

This is not the school as your child will experience it if you sign him on. Turn up a few days later and you might find the plastic plants have been completely trashed! So it may be better to visit on an ordinary working day, rather than attending one of these pre-planned events. And if you really want to get a feel for the atmosphere, try to visit during morning break or at lunchtime. The playground, the corridors, the dining room – these are the places that tell you what a school is really like.

And don't just open your eyes, open your ears too. Schools are never the quietest of places, and it would be worrying if all the children were working in absolute silence. But there's a difference between a creative buzz and an unholy din. Evidence shows that too much noise is detrimental to children's learning. Average sound levels in school are about seventy decibels; the same as a busy road junction. Research at London's Institute of Education found that when the noise level rises to between ten and forty decibels higher than that, the school's test scores fall to 30 per cent lower than average. That noise doesn't just include children chatting, teachers talking and the rustle of crisp packets. It often includes noise pollution from outside, beyond the school's control. Schools by busy roads or directly under flight paths need to be well soundproofed. Otherwise teachers and children will raise their voices, even subconsciously, until the background babble reaches a point where it's difficult to concentrate or hear properly, and where learning suffers.

Finally, if you visit a school, be sure to chat to the teachers and children. Ask questions about work, or about the displays on the wall. It's not the answers you're interested in, it's the way people interact with you. Do staff seem stressed, or are they relaxed and approachable? Are children open and friendly, or rude and wary? If you have concerns about a school, don't be afraid to visit on more than one occasion – perhaps at different times of the day – to make sure you're getting the true picture. When you're buying a house, you'll call in or drive by several times to make sure it's the one for you. Think of school-hunting along the same lines as house-hunting, and you'll be in the right frame of mind.

Things To Do

- If you're looking at several schools, try to visit them close together. That way it's easier to make comparisons.
- Always ask, 'Are there any parts of the school I haven't seen?' Guided visits often steer you away from bits of the school that may be run-down.

- Ask the head teacher and senior staff what vision they have for the future and what they think their school will be like in five years' time.
- Make notes after the visit, listing what you liked and didn't like about the school. Get your child to do the same. Then compare.

THE POSTCODE LOTTERY

You've done your research. You've got all the right information and asked all the right questions. You've identified which school you like best.

But that's only the start. Now you have to secure your child a place there. If the school isn't full then there shouldn't be a problem. You have the right to state a preference for *any* school, not just your nearest one. But the best schools are popular – and that means a scramble for places.

So how do oversubscribed schools decide who to let in, and who to turn away?

The problem is, there's no hard-and-fast rule for this. Different local authorities have different ways of doing things. And some schools, such as faith schools and academies, can set their own admissions procedure. But there are general rules, laid down by the government, about how maintained schools can choose their pupils – and how they can't.

Schools can't base their decision on the child's family circumstances, or family wealth. They can't offer children a place just because Mum's a teacher, Dad's a governor and they both help out at the jumble sale. They can't use an interview with a child as a sneaky way of finding out how bright he is. They can't base their decision on reports from another school about a child's work or behaviour. And they can't select children on a first-come, first-served basis, according to the order the applications came in.

So what does that leave? What can schools do? Well, they

can give priority to children who already have a sister or brother at the school. Grammar schools, of course, can cherry-pick according to academic ability, and specialist secondary schools can select up to 10 per cent of pupils according to their 'aptitude' in the school's specialist subject. And it's fine if schools want to have a random lottery, and just pick names out of a hat, so long as it's all above board.

The other thing schools can do is to select by catchment area, giving places to children who live near the school. This is the most common selection procedure, and the most controversial. It's the one you might also find the most frustrating.

Around a hundred thousand people each year move house with the express purpose of being near a desirable school. Which is good news, of course, if you've got a house to sell – prices in sought-after catchment areas can be over 30 per cent higher than those just outside – but not for cash-strapped parents. Some of these have resorted to giving false addresses, or renting a house in the area for a few months, just so their application will be eligible. But popular schools have seen all the catchment cons before, and are on the lookout.

Did You Know?

- An ICM opinion poll has shown that 30 per cent of parents would consider moving house to get their child into their first-choice school.
- Meanwhile, 19 per cent would be willing to rent a property close to the school and 14 per cent would consider faking an address.

Before you go running down to the estate agents – be warned. Even living within litter-blowing distance of a school may not be enough. Catchment areas of successful schools are shrinking all the time. They can be reduced year on year to keep numbers manageable, and sometimes extend just a few hundred metres from the gates. And schools can't, and won't, guarantee places even to children living in the catchment area. This is especially true if you move in the middle of a school year, or outside the usual intake times. If the school is full, then it's full. It won't matter where you live: you could still miss out.

Because this can all be confusing and stressful, many local authorities now have people whose job it is to offer advice to parents who are in the process of choosing a school. These 'choice advisers' are the people with the best knowledge about the specific situation in your area. They can tell you whether a school is usually oversubscribed, what the selection procedures are, and whether or not your child has a realistic chance of being offered a place. They can advise about possible alternatives, and help you to draw up your list of preferred schools in such a way as to ensure that you at least get one of your choices. So if you're feeling dazed and disheartened, they might be a good port of call.

Even if you can afford to buy your way into a desirable area with a successful school, you may want to pause for thought. It all comes back to the question of what makes a school 'good'. Does it get outstanding results because it's a wonderful place of learning? Or does it do well because it takes in children from wealthy areas? Do schools shape children? Or do children shape schools? It may well be that the school most parents see as desirable, isn't actually the best one for your child. Do your research carefully – and don't be afraid to make your own decisions, rather than just following the herd.

6. KNOWING THE SYSTEM: DIFFERENT TYPES OF SCHOOL AND HOW THEY WORK

Ellie's parents have read in the paper about a new academy opening in their area. At the moment, Ellie goes to the local primary, but it will soon be time to move on. Some of her friends are going to independent schools, some are off to the nearby comprehensive. But maybe the academy will be better? Ellie's parents are baffled by the range of schooling on offer, and find the jargon confusing. They just want to know what will suit Ellie best.

It's not easy to decide which school will be best for your child. There's more choice than ever before. In many ways, that's a good thing. But it can also make life complicated. Independent or maintained? Faith or secular? Selective or mixed-ability? It's important to know exactly how each type of school is run, what they offer, and whether or not they will get results.

INDEPENDENT SCHOOLS

Let's start by talking money. Independent schools aren't cheap. Average fees are around £8,000 a year and, taking inflation into account, educating a child privately from the age of five through to the age of eighteen will set you back almost £150,000. And that's just an averagely priced independent day school. For boarding, you can double those numbers. For the likes of Eton, Harrow and Winchester, you can almost treble them. In fact, latest figures show that over a hundred schools in the UK now charge more than £20,000 a year.

There are cheaper options. In recent years, private companies have been busy setting up a number of cut-price independent schools. They promise high-quality teaching, but without the lavish facilities of the top private schools. If your child can live without the swimming pool and fancy cricket pavilion then fees start at around £4,000 per year. And there are usually deferred-payment schemes where you make reduced payments over longer periods of time, to help ease the burden.

Even so, it's hardly bargain basement. £4,000 a year can buy a very nice holiday, not to mention a new bathroom or kitchen. Yet independent schools aren't short of customers. The number of children educated privately has grown year on year for the last decade and currently stands at around 600,000 – or 7 per cent of the school-age population. And surveys suggest that around half of all parents would choose a private school if they could afford the fees.

Did You Know?

- Educating a child at an independent school can cost over £150,000.
- A child at an independent school is four times more likely to get an A grade than a child at a maintained school.

The obvious question is this: why are so many parents willing to fork out a fortune when they could send their child to the local comprehensive for free? Because some people are so rich that this kind of money is just a drop in the ocean? Perhaps. Because it's been a family tradition for generations? In some cases. Yet over 40 per cent of parents who send their children to private schools are what the Independent Schools Council calls 'first-time buyers' – people who were themselves educated in the state sector but who choose to go private for their children. And many of them make considerable sacrifices in order to pull together the fees. So, what's the big attraction?

Well, in 2005, over half of all GCSE exams sat by independent-school pupils resulted in an A or A* grade. This compares to just 13 per cent in the state sector. Put another way, children in the independent sector are four times as likely to get a top grade. It's a similar story at A/S and A2 level. And independent-school pupils seem to be virtually guaranteed a place at university, with almost 95 per cent of leavers heading into higher education.

Critics of private education argue that these sort of results are simply a reflection of the fact that most of the pupils come from middle-class homes, with supportive parents who push them to achieve. But fans of independent schools say the success is the consequence of high-quality teaching. Private schools offer higher salaries and more relaxed working conditions than most maintained schools, so they find it easier to attract, and retain, the best teachers. The Independent Schools Council also points to an average ratio of one teacher to every ten pupils, which means children are taught in smaller classes and are more likely to receive one-to-one assistance.

But parents who choose to pay quite often feel that getting their child better exam results is only part of the attraction. The cheque for the termly fees buys more, they believe, than a few grade As. It buys an all-round package: a nice, clean and comfortable environment; an emphasis on good manners and respect for teachers; and a whole raft of extra-curricular opportunities. On a visit to one of the country's leading public schools, the head teacher cheerily admitted that when parents saw his dazzlingly green playing fields, purpose-built theatre and state-of-the-art sports hall they were usually happy to sign on the dotted line, without asking too many questions about the school's academic standards.

It's all very well to make the most of good facilities. If your child is a budding actor or a champion athlete in the making, then she may well benefit from having a theatre to rehearse in or a decent track to train on. But if you want value for money, then you need to know the teaching is up to scratch as well as the cricket pavilion. Do independents guarantee high-quality teaching in the classroom? The answer is that many independent schools are outstanding. They are dynamic, progressive and forward thinking, and they make good use of their independence, and the fact that they're not bound by the latest government initiatives. But a significant minority are fairly awful. Assume nothing, and be sure to do your research.

For a start, it's worth remembering that guaranteeing good results isn't always the same thing as providing a good education. Some independent schools are quite happy to 'spoon-feed' children to ensure a clutch of top grades and satisfy parents that their £10,000 a year has been well spent. But this will do nothing to help them become creative thinkers and learners, and may in fact be a disadvantage when they progress on to university or work. Ask questions about how and why pupils are learning, not just what they're learning. And if the school seems in many respects like the one you went to, don't just reminisce: be wary. It may be that their teaching methods are old-fashioned and could do with a shot in the arm.

And when you're looking at local independents, find out about how they are funded and run. Schools do go bust, and it can be extremely disruptive, especially if your child is in an exam year. If the school is well established, it is likely that it will be run as a charity, probably on the basis of some ancient trust fund. Surplus income will be ploughed back into the school, and the fees paid by parents will probably be supplemented by other forms of income. Be on your guard if you find the school is run commercially, for profit. Education isn't a business, and it's very rare for this kind of school to be a success.

More good news about schools run as charities is that, in order to hang on to charitable status, they have to work hard to be accessible and inclusive. This may mean the school is active in the community, building up all kinds of partnerships with other local schools or organisations. And it will almost certainly mean there will be scholarships and bursaries on offer. These work in different ways, depending on the school. Some will be means-tested, some ability-tested, and some a combination of both. It's a two-way deal. The school pays a large part of your child's fees, or even lets them in for free. In return, your kid notches up dozens of A-grade exam results and strolls into Oxford or Cambridge. Cue lots of nice pictures in the local press and a priceless boost to the school's reputation. Around one in three children at independent schools is on some kind of bursary or scholarship, meaning that while a private education is by no means available to all, it's possibly more accessible than many parents imagine.

GRAMMAR SCHOOLS, SETTING AND STREAMING

Fill up a classroom with bright, hard-working children and good things will happen. Positive peer pressure, healthy competition, that kind of thing. Which explains why grammar schools are so popular. You thought they'd died out? Not at all. More children are now taught in academically selective schools than was the case twenty years ago. In the last decade, numbers have risen by more than a third. Around one in twenty children go to a grammar.

But do grammar schools offer a better education? If you're looking to turn a child into a high-flyer then the idea seems sound. You have to be smart to get in. You get put in a class with lots of other smart children. And you all zip merrily through the syllabus without having to wait for the dunces at the back to catch up.

The evidence, however, is patchy. As you'd expect, grammar schools usually come well up the league tables. But some top-performing comprehensives actually do better than some grammar schools. And a recent study by the National Foundation for Educational Research shows that very able pupils make better progress in comprehensives, with selective schools being of most benefit to 'borderline' pupils who only just squeeze in.

In the end, whether selective or non-selective is best is probably a marginal decision. It's likely to boil down to the personality of individual children. A brainy child in a non-selective school may get more attention than if they're just one of dozens of bright kids at a grammar school. On the other hand, if a child is inclined to be lazy, a comprehensive may offer more opportunity for hiding away and coasting along.

Some people object to grammar schools on the grounds that they siphon off the cleverest children in an area, so the other schools suffer. But others would argue that having one school that caters for academic high-flyers, and perhaps another school that suits children who want vocational options, is good common sense. It allows schools to specialise.

Whatever your view on grammars, they're only an option if you live in certain parts of the country. There are no grammar schools at all in Wales or Scotland, and of the 164 in England, most are in the southeast. And even if you do live in a grammar school area, you should be aware that your child will face stiff competition to get in. In 2006, there were ten applicants for every grammar school place.

Even if your child is not at a grammar school, the chances are that she will still come across a form of selection. Just because a school is non-selective in general doesn't mean it won't try to group its most able children together for at least some of the time. In fact, government policy is for all secondary schools to use setting, unless they can justify their decision not to. As it happens, some schools still prefer to teach children in mixed-ability classes, while many schools set in certain subjects but not others. So which approach gets the best results?

Unfortunately, the reason different schools do different things is that no one has come up with a definitive answer. The argument for setting seems a strong one. In mixed-ability groups, the teacher often ends up aiming for the middle ground. It means the top children don't get stretched and the weaker ones get left behind. But studies have shown that the impact of setting on exam results is minimal, and that what little effect it does have tends to be negative, because it de-motivates those children outside the top group.

When picking the best school for your child, it's worth asking about the school's approach to setting. How do they set – and why? Many schools use setting as a matter of practicality, rather than out of educational principle. For example, some GCSE subjects offer a choice between 'foundation' and 'higher' exam papers, so it makes sense for schools to group together pupils sitting the same paper. But be wary of schools that set children into general ability groups which are then applied to every subject, rather than setting on a subject-by-subject basis. Most children are stronger in some areas than others and this kind of general streaming is almost always bad news.

In any case, some schools are now taking more innovative approaches to setting. For example, at Brooke Weston City Technology College in Northamptonshire, children in each class can choose between four levels of work: basic, standard, extended and advanced. It's the children themselves who choose which level to tackle. At other schools, the idea of setting within year groups has been extended to group together children from different years who are working at a similar level.

If setting does exist at your child's school, find out whether or not the sets are reviewed on a regular basis. After all, children advance at different speeds, and the system needs to be flexible – though it often isn't. Being in the wrong group can cause problems. If your child gets ahead, she'll get bored. If she falls behind, she'll become frustrated. The biggest mistake you can make is to pester the school into promoting your child to a higher set. Teachers are in the best position to judge, and they get it right most of the time.

SPECIALIST SCHOOLS

Specialist schools and colleges are secondary schools that claim a particular area of strength. It could be languages, technology, sport, arts, maths or science. It doesn't mean they don't do all the other subjects as well, just that they think they're particularly good in one area.

To gain specialist status, these schools have to raise money through private sponsorship. If they do, the government gives them an even larger pot of money. The result of this extra funding is usually some top-notch facilities, relating to the area in which the school has chosen to specialise. But don't be fooled into thinking specialist schools are very, very special: they are now, in fact, the norm, outnumbering non-specialist ones by around eight to one. And soon it's hoped that all schools will have specialist status, meaning an end to 'bog-standard' comprehensives.

There's plenty of evidence that specialist schools have helped to raise standards. Overall, their GCSE results are slightly better than those of non-specialist schools, and in their specialist subject the gap is usually wider. Specialist schools are helped by the fact that they have the right to select a proportion of their pupils according to their 'aptitude' in the chosen area. In other words, they can be selective, although many specialist colleges decline to take advantage of this.

If you look around, you'll probably find a choice of specialist schools in your area. But when you're deciding which school is best for your child, this can sometimes just confuse the issue.

How important is it to take a school's specialist subject into account? Well, it may sound obvious, but it probably depends how specialised your child is. If she shows real talent in drama, then seeking out a performing arts college would seem like a sensible move. If you can't drag her away from the home chemistry kit, then take a good look at the specialist science college.

Don't automatically assume that specialist colleges represent unqualified excellence. And remember that the choice you make when your child is ten or eleven will determine what happens for quite a few years to come. So just because she's into chemistry at the age of ten, doesn't mean she might not decide in a couple of years that poetry is actually the thing for her. Many schools have more than one area of strength, even if it's not emblazoned in the school title. A specialist language college, for example, might also offer excellent performing arts teaching and facilities. But perhaps there was already a performing arts college in the area, so they chose languages as their 'official' specialist subject. In other words, it's important to look beyond the label of a school, and find out where exactly its strengths and weaknesses lie. In most cases your child will be much better off getting a good all-round education, rather than being packed off to a school that is strong in one area, but weak in all the others. After all, any school worth its salt will promote excellence in all areas, not just one or two.

ACADEMIES

Even if you haven't got one near you, you'll have heard about academies. They're in the news. They're controversial. There are currently around a hundred of these schools either already open, or under development. And there are plans to at least double that number.

Academies are often described as 'independent state schools'. They are funded, mostly, by the taxpayer and they don't charge fees. In that sense, they are state schools. But in other ways they are independent. They are outside the control of the local authority. They can set their own rules and admissions policy. They can choose the kind of education they want to provide, and what areas they want to specialise in.

> ### Did You Know?
> - The first academies opened in 2002. The target is for there to be 200 by 2010. There are none in Wales or Scotland.
> - Private sponsors donate £2 million, but the average cost of an academy is more than ten times that amount. The rest of the money comes from the government.
> - At several academies the number of children getting five GCSEs at grades A to C has more than doubled.

The controversy is around the need for academies to find a private sponsor or benefactor, who ploughs some of his or her own money into the project. Two million pounds is about the going rate. In return, the sponsor gets to sit on the governing body, choose the head teacher, and determine the direction of the school. Critics argue that allowing people to buy control of a school is a risky business. They worry that sponsors may be motivated by a desire to indoctrinate children into a particular way of thinking and point to the fact that, so far, around a third of all academies have been sponsored by religious foundations, many of them evangelical or creationist groups.

In fact the indoctrination issue probably isn't worth getting too worked up about. Academies may have some flexibility about what they teach, but they're still subject to inspections, and they're not allowed to stray too far from the national curriculum. The sponsor certainly has a good deal of influence, but so does the chair of governors at any school in the country.

The real question is whether academies are actually any better than an ordinary school. And this is difficult to judge. Academies often replace schools that are failing or have serious problems. That means two things. Firstly, it means most academies do better than the schools they replace. An injection of cash, a fresh start and some new direction is just what these schools need. Improvement is almost inevitable. But it also means that many academies don't perform well when compared to other schools around the country. There are usually good reasons why the original school was failing, and it's not possible to turn things round overnight. So critics and supporters of academies can both find plenty of evidence to back up their case.

Some academies draw pupils from far and wide. Others draw only from the local community. Some academies select pupils according to ability, others according to faith, others according to where pupils live. Nearly all of them are proving popular with parents, and many of them are oversubscribed. Just 57 children wanted a place at the TP Riley school in Walsall in the year before it closed. When it was replaced by Walsall Academy, there was a scramble for places, with more than 500 applications in the first year.

If you have the option of an academy, the best advice is to view it in the same way as any other school. Most academies are well funded, and have excellent new facilities. Many have been built from scratch, and look very impressive. But at the end of the day, academies are not that different to ordinary schools. They might be good, they might be bad, they might be indifferent. So don't be taken in by the rebranding and the flashy title. Look at what the school is really like.

FAITH SCHOOLS, BIG SCHOOLS, LITTLE SCHOOLS

There's not such a variety of primary school options as secondary. But you still need to know the ins and outs of the system. It's true that results at GCSE and A level are what shape a child's future, but the foundations for success are laid down long before then.

The factor most likely to shape the character of a state primary school is whether it's a faith school or a secular or community one. There are over 18,000 primary schools up and down the country, and around 6,000 of them are faith schools. Given that only one in twelve people in the UK goes to church, it's surprising that one in three primaries are faith-based. But the popularity of church schools often has less to do with religion, and more to do with results. Roman Catholic and Church of England schools make up a third of all primaries, but account for two-thirds of the top-hundred-performing schools. That explains why faith schools are popular with parents of all faiths, or no faith at all. As a group, only independent schools get better results. Let us pay. Let us pray. It's your choice.

Did You Know?

- There are almost 7,000 faith schools in the UK. They include Anglican, Catholic, Methodist, Sikh, Muslim, Jewish, Seventh Day Adventist, Creationist and Greek Orthodox.
- Most faith schools get better-than-average results, with Anglican schools doing particularly well.

It's hard to put a finger on just why faith schools are so successful. There are acts of collective worship. Religious education has a high profile. And the governing body is usually controlled by a church or faith group. Beyond that, faith schools aren't really very different to other maintained schools. They are at least 90 per cent funded by the local authority, so it's not a case of them having better resources.

Many people think faith schools do well because they have a reputation for embodying values of discipline, order and family commitment. This means parents are keen to send their children there, and a good reputation breeds success.

Admissions policies at church schools vary, but, not surprisingly, they often have something to do with going to church. Some faith schools only accept children of that particular faith. Roman Catholic primaries, for example, tend to have quite strict admissions policies and will sometimes ask for proof that you have been a regular churchgoer for at least four years. Church of England schools tend to be more open and are often happy to admit children of all faiths, but policy varies from school to school. Some new Church of England schools make a quarter of places available to children of other faiths. But others give priority to families that are committed churchgoers, meaning they should attend a service at least twice a month.

The other major difference between primaries is size: some primary schools have more than a thousand children, others have fewer than thirty. Small schools tend to have a family atmosphere, which may suit some children better. They are more likely to get one-to-one attention, and the pastoral care will be excellent. But in very small schools children may be taught in mixed-age groups, which isn't always ideal. In larger primaries, a bigger staff means more specialist teachers. That can be particularly important in subjects like PE, music or art. If your child is turning into a bright young thing, it also means more competition to spur them on. Large schools also offer better salaries so they often attract better-quality teachers. Heads of big primaries are paid double what heads of the smallest schools get.

Of course, the size of your local primaries will depend on where you live. Schools tend to be smaller in remoter, rural areas, and larger in cities. So you may well find all the primaries within a reasonable travelling distance are more or less the same size. If you *do* have a choice between a small school and a larger one, then you'll need to weigh up the pros and cons. It will probably come down to the personality of your child, and the kind of atmosphere that will suit them best.

7. GETTING UP TO DATE: TWENTY THINGS THAT ARE HAPPENING IN SCHOOLS TODAY

Abigail is 35, and her first child, Josh, leaves Year 6 next year. They spend a lot of time talking about what school Josh should go to next. Abigail had a great time herself at school, and she did well. She wants Josh to go to the same sort of school as she did. But Abigail left school nearly twenty years ago: the sort of school she went to doesn't exist any more.

As the world changes, so do schools. Your child's experience of school will probably be very different from your own. It may be that you think things were better in your day; that discipline was stricter and children better behaved; that standards were higher and exams tougher; that everyone worked harder and neater and quicker. But the reality is that schools have changed mostly for the better in recent years.

This chapter explains some of the things that have changed

since your day – even if 'your day' wasn't so very long ago. Not all these initiatives are happening in every school. Some schools will have different ideas, which are equally exciting. But it'll give you a flavour of what successful and progressive schools are doing, and this should give you some idea of how your own child's school measures up.

1: OPEN ALL HOURS

Schools used to be open from half-past eight in the morning until half-past three in the afternoon. And that was that. If you arrived at school early, you stood outside in the playground, shivering, and if you dawdled after the last bell the caretaker would come and chase you home.

But things are changing. Just as shops and supermarkets are open longer and later, so an increasing number of schools now operate outside traditional hours. These 'extended schools' provide a range of services, not just to pupils but to the whole community. They offer homework clubs and after-school activities. They make their ICT and sports facilities available to local people in the evenings. And they might run parenting classes, or offer health clinics. At Chessington Community College in Kingston, for example, the day starts at 7.30 a.m. for breakfast clubs and closes at 11 p.m. after people have left their adult education classes. On Saturdays, members of the local South Korean community run lessons in their native language. The sports facilities are open to local residents, and there is even a bar.

The number of extended schools is growing year on year. It's often a good way for schools to make money that they can plough back into facilities and a report by Ofsted in 2006 suggested that children at extended schools get improved results, because they feel more involved and more confident. But at the moment, the evidence for or against extending school opening hours is far from conclusive, and some schools are heading in the opposite direction by actually trying to shorten the working day. Government guidelines say schools should provide between 21 and 24 hours of teaching a week, but how they organise the day is up to them. So some are following the example of schools in European neighbours like Germany, where school traditionally starts early and finishes early. At Burnage High School in Manchester, for example, the timetable was restructured so lessons could finish at lunchtime. And at Queen's Park Community School in the London borough of Brent, lunch is served at 11.10 a.m. so the afternoon can get started earlier. Other schools have shortened the lunch break to as little as 25 minutes, to ensure an early finish.

But why? Because teachers think children work best in the morning. They are quieter, more focused and better behaved – so it makes sense to get as much teaching as possible done before lunch. It also means children get a longer break between one school day and the next, so they can get properly refreshed and relaxed, and it means more time, and more daylight, for after-school activities.

But not all experts are convinced. There are those who say that children are only better behaved in the mornings because their brains are less active. So while children may be livelier and noisier in the afternoon, that's also when they are likely to learn best.

2: MAKING TIME

Schools are also starting to be flexible about how they organise lessons. Some short, sharp half-hours may still remain, but they're likely to be mixed up with longer blocks of learning. This gives more time for in-depth learning and discussion, and means children are much more likely to become absorbed by what they're doing. It's also much better for organising group work or practical activities.

Evidence suggests both children and teachers may work better this way. At St John's School and Community College in

Wiltshire, for example, children in Years 7 and 8 study topics, rather than subjects. These topics are broad enough to include all kinds of things, from maths and science to art and history. So a typical topic might be 'What makes us unique?' It can run through several days or weeks, with subject specialists called in to teach a module relevant to the overall topic, such as human biology or the geography of cities. It helps children understand the links between different subjects, rather than seeing everything as stand-alone, and prepares them for the kind of diverse project-based tasks you often get in the workplace.

Special project weeks are also good for tackling creative challenges that might not fit into the usual timetable. Lots of schools set aside several days each term for children to work in groups on everything from composing a school anthem to recording a radio programme or building a totem pole. It gets children actively learning new skills, mixing with different people, and seeing school in a different light. So don't be afraid to enquire about timetable arrangements. Ask your child's school why they do things the way they do. And ask them if they've ever thought of doing things differently.

3: SUPERTEACHERS

Most teachers are good. Some are very good. But a few really stand out from the crowd. They're the kind of teachers who can inspire children and transform a school. Since 1998, these teachers have been able to apply for the title of Advanced Skills Teacher (AST). And in 2006 a new category was introduced – the Excellent Teacher.

These superteachers get paid more than ordinary teachers – and in return they share their skills by helping to advise other schools, and by giving model lessons that other teachers can observe. A potential salary of up to £60,000 helps attract top graduates to the profession, and keeps talented teachers in the classroom, instead of them taking jobs as deputies and heads.

But are these teachers really all that special? It would seem so. Advanced Skills Teachers make up just 1 per cent of the teaching workforce, but at last year's annual teaching awards, they carried off three of the national and nine of the regional prizes. So when you're looking at where to send your child, it may be worth asking how many of these superteachers a school has, and which subjects they teach. It's another benchmark, another form of quality control – if a school has several top-class teachers, then it's likely to be going places.

4: GOING GLOBAL

All schools teach children how to be good citizens. And the best schools teach them not just about the local community, but about the global community. This means more than poring over maps on the classroom wall. It means having a 'link' with a partner school in another country and sharing lessons and projects. Having strong links with partner schools is a sure sign that a school is outward looking. And with email, webcams and satellite links, there's no excuse for schools to shut themselves off from the rest of the world.

Having links with overseas schools helps pupils in the UK get a sense of perspective. It teaches them how others live. If the link is with a school in the developing world, it can raise awareness of important issues such as poverty and water shortage. It can make children more responsible and less self-centred. Well-established links offer opportunities for groups to visit the partner school and experience life differently.

Links can also be a helpful resource for teachers. Many schools organise festivals exploring things like the food or dance or family cultures of a partner school. Others work with partners in the developing world to create lessons for subjects like art and geography, while partners from Spain to Japan can be useful for learning languages.

There's a lot of lip service paid to linking, so delving a bit deeper into how it works at your child's school might be a good indication of how active the school is outside of the usual curriculum. It should be about more than a quick whip-round at Christmas for a school in Africa. Polesworth School in Staffordshire, for example, has partners in China, India, Ghana, Poland, Spain and Germany – and organises exchange visits for staff and pupils. Nearly all the children at Polesworth are white, so it gives them a valuable insight into other cultures and ways of life, and helps prepare them for life at university and beyond. But effective links don't have to be with faraway places. Highfields School in Matlock works closely with Bemrose, an inner-city school in Derby – so that children from the country can mix with children from a more urban environment. Good schools always try to broaden children's horizons.

5: TERMS AND CONDITIONS

Most schools still have three terms each year. One leading up to Christmas, one leading up to Easter, and one leading up to the summer break, which starts in mid-July. But not everyone thinks that's the best way to organise things. It means the autumn term is much longer than the other two terms. Teachers get tired. So do children. Time is lost to sickness. Then there's the length of the summer holiday. Taking six or seven weeks off school is a nice idea. But research shows that many children take a backwards step over the summer, forgetting some of what they've learned. At the start of the next term teachers then have to spend time going over old ground. The other problem with the three-term calendar is that, because Easter moves around, the dates of the summer term vary. And that means teachers can be caught out, and have to hurry to get through the syllabus before the exams start.

So some schools have tried out new systems. Some have tried taking a week off the summer holidays and adding it to the October half-term, to stop everyone getting so run-down. Other schools, such as Woodlands Primary in Lincolnshire, have been more radical – dividing the year into five terms, of eight weeks each. There is a two-week break between terms, with a four-week holiday in the summer. Research by Professor Trevor Kerry of the University of Lincoln shows that pupils in schools such as Woodlands feel the five-term year helps their concentration and improves their test scores. The only downside is that they keep getting picked up by truant patrols!

6: BLOG, BLOG, BLOG . . .

Pinning a child's work to the classroom wall used to be a good way of making them proud and keeping them motivated. But it's even more of a thrill to see their work up there on the Internet, for anyone to look at. Some schools encourage children to keep online diaries, which is a great way of getting them writing. Others help children set up web pages to showcase their project work. Or get them to produce online newspapers. Or encourage them to produce video clips for YouTube. One primary school in London even hired a professional camera crew to help the children make a documentary about school assemblies, which featured on Channel 4's website.

It doesn't really matter what the task is. Children love to see their work on show – and there's no bigger stage than the worldwide web.

7: PUPIL POWER

Pupil power is on the rise. Young people want their opinions to be heard – and more and more schools are listening. In Wales, schools are obliged to have a student council. In the rest of the UK, more and more schools are choosing to set one up, so children can have a say in their own education.

A school council consists of a group of pupils, usually elected by their classmates. They meet to discuss everything from how lessons are taught, to what's on the menu at mealtimes. Councils aren't anything new – they've been around since the

1970s. What's changed is that schools are now taking notice of what the council says, and making changes accordingly. School councils now have real power.

Asking whether your child's school has a council, and finding out how it operates, can tell you a great deal about the attitudes of the head teacher. The best schools are democratic places, where children are listened to and respected. A good council encourages children to be involved, and helps them to become independent. It also helps to improve behaviour: children are more likely to follow rules that have been laid down by their peers, rather than ones which have been forced upon them by the school.

School councils can help make their school a success. Ofsted inspectors take school councils seriously and always listen to their views. And some schools even involve their councils in selecting new teachers, allowing them to interview candidates and say which they prefer.

From my experience, schools that have a strong, active council tend to be happy places where children are encouraged to take the initiative, instead of being spoon-fed by their teachers. They are places where children become confident and articulate. They are almost always good schools.

8: SMART SCHOOLS

Draughty mobile classrooms, smelly toilets and crowded corridors can make school an unpleasant experience. They can make it hard for staff and pupils to concentrate; they can be noisy and cold. And it's hard to motivate children if lessons are being taught in crumbling buildings. Fortunately, the last five years have seen a decent level of investment in school buildings – with more to come.

Not all schools have spent their money in the same way. Where some have simply rebuilt or refurbished along traditional lines, others have been bolder and more imaginative. Newly built schools sometimes resemble fancy corporate headquarters, with thickly carpeted floors and leafy plants in the corridors. They tend to be well ventilated and well lit, with lots of natural light. Some schools have been built as a series of small units, almost like villages, rather than having children lumped together in one huge building.

High on the schools' shopping list has been ICT, so that classrooms have been equipped with computers, Internet connections and interactive whiteboards. A rare few even provide individual learning terminals for every pupil. But sometimes it's the low-tech solutions that make the difference. Many schools have opted for classrooms with moveable walls, allowing children to work in small groups, or as a whole class. And schools that genuinely value their pupils' wellbeing have invested in desks and chairs that can be adjusted for children of different heights. A minor point? Perhaps. But children sit on school chairs for 15,000 hours of their life – and according to the charity BackCare as many as half of all children suffer back pain as a result of poor seating.

So does fancy design really make a difference when it comes to results? Is your child more likely to succeed in a shiny new school? Well, looks aren't everything of course, and heavy investment in buildings may be covering the cracks at a struggling school. But it may be worth paying some attention to the physical state of corridors and classrooms. Kingsdale School in Southwark, for example, was recently remodelled at a cost of £11 million – and in the next three years it saw the number of pupils getting five A to C grades at GCSE rise from 15 per cent to 41 per cent. Other schools report a similar experience. If children are comfortable in their environment and proud of their school, they're more likely to be positive about their work.

9: GETTING CONNECTED

Good schools give children as much contact as possible with the real world. In fact, good schools are part of the real world, not separate from it. When children go on a visit to the theatre, or meet a successful businessman, it can give them a new outlook or spark their own career aspirations. Working for a day, a week, or even a term with an artist or writer can be inspirational. Getting an insight into how companies work, spending some time on the shop floor or in the office, or setting up small pupil-based enterprises can build confidence and aspiration. Getting to grips with a sporting passion in the heart of a local sports club can give a child a real boost.

More than ever, it's important for a school to be well connected. Many heads and governors spend a good deal of time and effort fostering useful contacts in the local community. It's nearly always time well spent. If there's nothing more at your child's school than a reporter from the local rag opening the annual fun day, then you should be asking why.

10: DATA TRACKING

Gone are the days when the only way of finding out how your child was doing was to wait for the end-of-year report. Most schools now chart progress on a weekly (or even daily) basis, using highly sophisticated data-management systems. Every grade for every piece of work in every subject can be logged centrally onto a computer. If a child's work dips below their usual standard, even for a week or two, the system alerts teachers that there could be a problem.

And it isn't just academic grades that get analysed – teachers can also enter information about attendance and behaviour. Perhaps a child is often absent on a Monday, or behaves poorly in one particular subject. If a pattern emerges, then the system will pick up on it.

These kinds of systems are a useful way of highlighting areas where schools might need to improve. Data tracking gives head teachers a detailed picture of how their school is functioning. It may be there's a problem with one particular year group, or that some teachers are clearly getting better results than others. The school can get the best teachers to share the secrets of their success, or get the less successful ones to attend some appropriate training days.

Best of all, the data allows schools to set realistic targets for both pupils and staff. At Albion Primary in Southwark, all teachers meet regularly with the assessment co-ordinator to discuss the latest data. Targets are set for each class, which are displayed on the classroom wall, and each pupil has individual targets fixed to their desk. It keeps everyone focused and motivated!

11: SOCRATES FOR SIX-YEAR-OLDS

In France, philosophy is an established part of the school curriculum. Here in the UK, getting children to ponder life's big questions is optional, but more and more schools are trying it. Most of them follow a programme known as Philosophy for Children. It's a movement that started in the US, but in the last five years it's caught on here – and there are now over 5,000 primary and secondary teachers trained to deliver the programme.

Philosophy lessons encourage children to think beyond the obvious, to debate issues and to consider the views of others. Children consider questions such as 'Is it ever OK to lie?' and 'Should people be made to give money to charity?' They have to back up their arguments, and be willing to change their minds. Research carried out in 2000 by Elizabeth Doherr, a clinical psychologist based in Norwich, found that when British children between five and eight are taught philosophy, their way of thinking becomes equivalent to that of a typical twelve-year-old.

At Gallions Primary in inner-city Newham, east London, philosophy lessons were introduced after it was branded the worst-performing school in its area. Since then it's become one of the top five schools in the borough, and has been rated 'outstanding' by Ofsted. Teachers say that the philosophy lessons have helped children become better problem-solvers and better listeners.

12: TALENT SPOTTING

'Gifted and Talented' is a national scheme designed to identify and nurture children who show outstanding ability – which usually means that they must be in the top 5 per cent for their age group nationally. The term 'gifted' refers to academic ability, while 'talented' is the word used for ability in sport or the arts.

It's the school's job to identify gifted and talented pupils, and then to make sure they get the necessary support to fulfil their potential. That may mean providing extra lessons, or one-to-one tuition, or arranging appropriate visits for the child, perhaps to museums or art galleries. Or it might involve putting the family in touch with outside organisations that may be able to help, such as local sports clubs, or youth theatres.

There's also a national academy for gifted and talented children at the University of Warwick. It's based on similar academies in the US and offers residential summer schools for high-flyers. Entry is dependent on a recommendation from your child's school, supported by good grades and test scores.

If you want to make sure your child's talents are well nurtured, then ask around about what schools are doing with the Gifted and Talented programme: some take it more seriously then others. Ofsted reckons around half of all schools are on top of their game in this respect. You need to make sure your child's school actively tries to spot talent. Ability isn't always obvious, and it's not enough to just look at test scores. The best schools are continuously on the lookout for children who may have hidden depths, and who may need more of a challenge to bring the best out of them.

13: PRIZES AND PUNISHMENTS

At one time, schools focused more on what children did wrong than on what they did right. There was plenty of stick, and not a great deal of carrot. Nowadays most teachers understand that offering praise and rewards is an effective way to motivate young people.

Taking a closer look at how a school uses sanctions and rewards can tell you a great deal about how it values its students. Increasingly schools are trying to use fewer punishments and to seem less authoritarian. School rules are being replaced by school 'values' or 'principles', which are general statements about the need to respect others. Good schools tend to have a clear system of sanctions – it's never left to the whim of individual teachers. They try to make the punishment fit the crime. They avoid making children do pointless tasks, like line-writing, and instead get them to perform tasks that are useful and constructive. They avoid giving punishments that will cause resentment by dragging on over a long period of time. They never punish a whole class just because they can't identify a guilty individual. And they never, ever humiliate children by forcing them to stand in a corner, or sit with their hands on their head.

Most schools operate some kind of rewards system, to celebrate achievement and good behaviour. Teachers might award points, cards, stamps, smiley faces, or even pebbles in a jar. Some schools take a high-tech approach, and children have swipe cards that store merit marks electronically.

And don't be surprised if your child lands a prize for their good marks. Usually, this will be CD tokens or cinema tickets, but some schools really go to town. They might offer MP3 players, driving lessons or even chauffeur-driven limousine rides to the end-of-year prom. At Denefield School in Reading, prizes have included flying lessons, hot-air balloon rides, snowboarding, surfing and makeovers. And some schools find that nothing beats hard cash when it comes to getting children motivated. Last year, Bristol Academy rewarded GCSE pupils with a total of £37,000 under its incentives scheme. Pupils were paid £10 for reaching predicted grades in each subject and £5 for every grade above that. Since the school introduced the incentive scheme the proportion of pupils gaining five or more good GCSEs has doubled.

You might find your local head teacher takes a more old-fashioned approach. Some still believe that praise should be its own reward and that children should be motivated by a love of learning and a desire to do well, not by vouchers, tokens and five-pound notes. The main thing is that there should always be a clear, well-thought-out policy. Effective use of sanctions and rewards can transform the whole atmosphere of a school.

14: OWN WORK, NOT HOMEWORK

All too often, work set to be done at home is tedious and unimaginative. Learn for a test. Do some exercises like the ones we did in class. Read the next chapter in the textbook – and take notes. But some schools are starting to see homework as a great chance to give children a free rein. At Cardiff High School, for example, formal homework has been scrapped, and children have time to pursue projects of their own choosing. Some of them choose to write a novel, deliver a PowerPoint presentation to the rest of the class, or create works of art, crafted over several weeks.

If children see homework as something to look forward to, rather than a chore, then they'll spend far more time and energy on their activities than if they were doing a set piece of work. Don't just presume your child should be practising sums or spellings for homework. A school that has a more imaginative approach may well be imaginative in other areas too.

15: GETTING PERSONAL

Compulsory schooling started in 1872. Back then, the education system was narrow and rigid. And why wouldn't it be? Save for the privileged few, most school-leavers would end up working in the factories of the Industrial Revolution. Employers were looking for discipline, reliability and subservience. And maybe, just maybe, the ability to read and write. School was school, and children sank or swam.

Today schools recognise that all young people are individuals, with different skills and aptitudes, different personalities and ambitions. We are finally breaking away from the idea of a one-size-fits-all education – and moving towards what is sometimes called 'personalised learning'.

But what does personalised learning really mean?

Well, the reality is that it means different things in different schools.

To make learning truly personal, each child would have to follow her own programme of work as she liked and when she liked. And in a comprehensive with more than a thousand children, and perhaps fewer than seventy staff, this would soon result in chaos and collapse. Teachers have to look after a whole class, and they can't be expected to deliver thirty different lessons to thirty different children.

But good schools are trying out different ways of at least making learning more flexible. Often this means allowing children to work at their own speed so that no one gets rushed through a topic and no one sits kicking their heels when they could be learning. Increased use of ICT makes it possible for children to work at the pace that suits them best, with the teacher supervising. Some schools are even mixing up age groups. This allows high-flyers to be fast-tracked – working with older children so they aren't held back. And it gives weaker children time to get to grips with the work, rather than feeling a failure because the class has moved on before they've understood.

Personalised learning is also about giving children the most possible choice about which subjects they take, and what modules they study. It's about encouraging children to become independent, with lots of project work, where they do their own research. And it's about offering children a working environment that suits them – that feels personal, rather than impersonal. At St Vincent's Primary School in Birmingham, for example, children don't have a fixed seat but are free to move around the classroom. Some parts of the room are bright and businesslike, others mellow and moody. One area has music playing, another is quiet. There are traditional desks and chairs, as well as comfy beanbags and sofas. Every child is encouraged to find the working conditions that suit them best. The result? Better behaviour and an improved attitude to work.

16: IT'S GOOD TO TALK

Schools are more caring places than they used to be. Most are on the lookout for any telltale signs that a pupil might be struggling or unhappy, and most teachers realise that happy children are more likely to work well.

One way of helping children who have difficulties, either academically or in their personal lives, is through teaming them up with a mentor: someone who is on hand to give advice, offer support or lend an ear. The mentor is usually a volunteer role model, perhaps from a local business or sports team, who gives up an hour or so a week, free of charge, and who is trained to encourage and listen to the child they work with. Meetings usually take place in school, during school hours, but there are exceptions: Sawtry Community College in rural Cambridgeshire has invested £10,000 in video-conferencing facilities so that local businessmen can mentor children without having to spend valuable time travelling out to the school.

Many schools are also training pupils to act as mentors to each other. This is known as peer mentoring, and it is usually older pupils who mentor younger ones, offering them the benefit of their experience. Peer mentoring is especially useful when children face a school-related problem, such as bullying.

The peer mentors offer confidential advice, and know where to turn if someone needs more specialist or qualified help. It can be a good way of getting different year groups to talk to each other, and of dispelling myths and rumours. If your child is chatting to a peer mentor you may not even know about it, but if you do, don't assume it's a sign that he's struggling. He may just enjoy talking things through with someone close to his own age. He may have a couple of niggling things to get off his chest. Usually, it's a good sign. Research has shown that when children team up with a mentor, they often become more confident and motivated – and their results improve sharply.

Alongside mentoring schemes, most schools have access to a counsellor. These are not the same as mentors: they are trained professionals employed by the school. Some pupils are referred to the counsellor by their teachers, but most schools also offer a drop-in service, where children can call by and talk to the counsellor about whatever is bothering them, in total confidence. Just the kind of thing we could all do with from time to time, and as proof of this a group of Edinburgh primary schools recently opened up their counselling services to parents as well as children.

It may be that your child never uses a mentor or a counsellor. It may be that his teachers provide all the pastoral support he needs. But it's good to check out what kind of provision is available: a reliable mentoring and counselling programme is a sure sign that a school has children's wellbeing at heart.

17: QUALIFIED FOR LIFE

Secondary education has always been a political football. In recent years there have been complaints that GCSEs and A levels are too easy; that exams are dumbed-down, so that results will go up. Others argue that our obsession with academic qualifications means children who are skilled in other ways don't get a chance to express themselves. Learning a trade is still seen as less desirable than going on to higher education, even though plumbers often have better job prospects – and bigger salaries – than many graduates.

The fourteen-to-nineteen curriculum is constantly being reviewed – and it's certain that things will change. But it's not clear quite how. In the meantime, some schools have got tired of government dithering and pushed ahead regardless, looking at ways of making learning more relevant and efficient.

Broadgreen High in Liverpool was one of the first schools in the UK to follow the International Baccalaureate (IB) instead of A levels. The advantage of the IB is that students study more subjects and become more rounded individuals. For example, even if you want to become a doctor, you'll still have to learn a foreign language. It also means students don't have to make career decisions too early. In Wales, schools now have the option of the Welsh 'bac', which operates along similar lines. And in Scotland, the exam system already allows children to study up to five subjects for their 'Highers'.

Other schools are finding ways to allow pupils to study vocational subjects alongside their GCSEs. Every week over 100,000 children in Years 10 and 11 are allowed time out of school to learn a trade. At Handsworth Grange School in Sheffield, for example, children can spend a day a week at the city's further education college, studying anything from hairdressing to car maintenance. Good schools are proving that it's possible to be flexible, and that there's more to life than GCSEs and A levels.

18: SAVING THE PLANET

The threat of global warming is a big issue for young people. And schools are doing their bit to teach children to respect the environment. Some head teachers have targeted the 'school run' by discouraging parents from driving their children to school. For example, many primaries organise a 'walking bus' in the mornings, so children can walk to school as part of a supervised group. And secondary schools are providing more safe storage for bikes, to encourage cyclists. At Kesgrave High near Ipswich, over 700 children arrive by bicycle each day.

Other schools lead the way on energy efficiency. Ilfracombe School in Devon has eight solar panels. Cassop Junior School in Durham is powered by an 18-metre-high wind turbine. And Kingsmead Primary School in Cheshire uses rainwater to flush the toilets. Many schools function as recycling points for the community – and an increasing number give space over to a vegetable patch, where children can grow organic produce.

Encouraging children to go green isn't necessarily going to improve literacy and numeracy. But it shows that some schools are taking a refreshingly rounded approach to education, instead of obsessing about SATs scores and league tables.

19: LEARN TO LEARN

Alongside lessons in maths, English and science, many schools now have lessons in learning.

But isn't learning what happens in every lesson?

Hopefully, yes. But children often learn without really understanding the mental processes involved. Schools that follow a 'Learning to Learn' programme teach pupils which parts of the brain are involved in different tasks, and how to use puzzles and games to 'wake up' the brain. Children learn the difference between shallow learning, where we know the facts, and deep learning, where we understand why the facts are important and how to apply them. They also learn what to do when they're stuck: how to think things through, and where to look for information.

In schools that value learning, the lessons aren't focused on the teacher, but on the learners. There's a strong emphasis on problem-solving, creative thinking, and role-play. There's evidence that teaching children learning and thinking skills leads to 'cognitive acceleration', where children are able to think in ways usually seen only in older age groups. Two programmes of work are particularly popular – CAME

(Cognitive Acceleration in Maths Education) and CASE (Cognitive Acceleration in Science Education) – and they both get impressive results, with children performing 15 to 20 per cent above average.

If you want your child to get ahead, ask what her school is doing when it comes to exploring learning skills. It may not be something she can pick up later: some experts believe that the best time for learning new ways of thinking is between the ages of twelve and fourteen, and that after the age of sixteen it becomes more difficult to change the way we think and work.

20: AND LEARN TO BE HAPPY

Extra-curricular activities used to mean signing up for the football team or learning lines for the school play. Things have moved on. Schools now offer after-school lessons in everything from circus skills to astronomy, ballroom dancing to bicycle maintenance. Some have as many as 150 activities a week to choose from, so there's more chance for everyone to find their niche.

And schools are thinking more carefully about how extra-curricular activities can enrich education, boost confidence and teach valuable skills like teamwork. Good schools are equipping children for life – instead of just getting them through their exams.

In some cases, this means looking to the future, perhaps offering Mandarin and Arabic lessons after hours, to go with the traditional French, German or Spanish taught during school. In other cases, it means a fresh approach to something more traditional. So at St Edmund's Girls' School in Salisbury, pupils can sign up for after-school lessons in good manners. They learn how to eat properly, the rules of polite conversation, how to dress for an interview, and how to make a good impression on other people.

Some schools are even tackling great big life-changing issues like how to be happy. At Wellington College in Berkshire, students have Life Skills lessons that focus on 'positive psychology'. The idea is that they'll learn something more important than trigonometry. Among other things, the lessons teach children the importance of a good night's sleep, how to cope when they're feeling sad, and how to make friends.

8. TOPPING UP OR OPTING OUT: SOME EXTRA CHOICES

Jake works hard at school. He is an able and motivated pupil. He is settled and happy. He has lots of friends and belongs to several after-school clubs. His parents don't want to disrupt him, but they feel he could be doing better. They believe he's not being stretched enough. They think he's not achieving as much as he could.

School is only one part of your child's education. It's a big part, but it's not everything. With the best will in the world, teachers can only do so much for your child. The rest may be down to you. So it's important to know the options for building on what happens in school.

PRIVATE TUTORS

The private tutor industry is booming. Almost a third of all eleven- to eighteen-year-olds have after-hours, one-to-one tuition at some point during their schooling. It could be just a session or two to clear up something they don't understand. It might be a helping hand with revision in the lead-up to exams. Or it might be on-going support over several years, designed to reinforce all the work done during school. But can tutoring really make a difference? And is it worth the extra cash?

In some parts of the country tutoring has almost become the norm. It can spread through a school like a virus. Once a large number of parents start buying one-to-one help for their children, others feel under pressure to follow suit. After all, they don't want their child to be at a disadvantage. Years ago, there was a stigma attached to needing extra support. Today, in some circles, a personal tutor is a must-have accessory. It's not just GCSE and A-level students who are getting help. Children as young as six now have private tuition. And in areas with grammar schools, coaching for the eleven-plus entrance test is a huge and growing market.

We're still some way behind other countries, though. In Hong Kong and Japan, for example, over 90 per cent of children have after-school tutoring. And in the US, some states run a voucher system, whereby if a school is deemed to be 'failing' parents are awarded tokens to spend on private tuition. In the UK, you have to foot the bill yourself. In most parts of the country tutors charge an hourly rate of between £15 and £20, while in London it may be nearer to £30. Not cheap. But some parents see it as a cut-price alternative to sending their child to private school. Buying three one-to-one lessons a week during term time will set you back around £1,500 a year. That's a lot of money – but still cheaper than the fees at an independent school.

When to use a tutor – and when not to

A personal tutor can have a hugely positive effect on your child's learning. They can boost confidence, enthusiasm and grades. But how much impact they have depends on two factors: how good the tutor is, and how well you make use of them. There are plenty of stories of lazy or incompetent tutors; of surly stubborn pupils who would rather be out skateboarding; or of unstructured lessons pushed into a noisy corner between the PlayStation and the hoovering. A waste of everyone's time, and your money. Research carried out at the Institute of Education has suggested that in general one-to-one tuition has little influence on exam results. The study found that having a private tutor only raised GCSE results by around half a grade.

So why don't tutors make more of a difference? Because very often their skills are not being used at the right time, in the right way. The reality is that there are certain situations where a tutor will make a great deal of difference, and other situations where they won't.

Did You Know?

- Researchers at the Institute of Education in London found one school where 65 per cent of GCSE students had extra tuition.
- Tutoring agencies say the fastest-growing area of business is in coaching primary school children for SATs and entrance tests.
- Maths tutors are in high demand. Of children who have private lessons, 70 per cent have tuition in maths. English is the next most popular subject.
- In some countries, private tuition is illegal. It's seen as giving an unfair advantage to richer families.

Tutoring works best when the idea comes from your child, rather than from you. But if you think your child needs extra help then try to raise the issue in a sensitive way. You don't want them to feel that it's a sign of failure. If your son or daughter keeps asking you for help, which you don't feel qualified to give, then that might be a good time to suggest a tutor. Point out that it's because of your own shortcomings, not theirs. Tutoring also works best when it's a long-term supplement, rather than a quick fix. That way your child can build up a working relationship with the tutor, and there's time for real progress to be made.

If your child has missed a lot of school through illness, then a tutor can help them catch up. If he is quiet in class or lacks confidence, then one-to-one attention can be useful. It allows him to ask questions and go at his own pace. If your child is struggling in one particular subject, then that's another time when tutoring could help. Perhaps he doesn't see eye-to-eye with the teacher in that subject. Perhaps he's simply got stuck with a bad teacher. Nearly every school has one. Many schools have more than one. A bad teacher may not be able to keep control of the class, they may not be up to speed with the syllabus, they may just be crossing off the days to their pension. Whatever the reasons, they're a menace to your child's education, and a good reason for bringing in some outside help. How do you know if your child has a bad teacher? Easy. He'll tell you. Kids aren't stupid. They know when a teacher is underprepared, lazy or cutting corners.

There are other good reasons for making use of tutors. One-to-one help can be an excellent way of stretching a gifted youngster. It can encourage a child to do better in his favourite subject, not just his weakest one. And tutoring needn't always be about better grades and results. It can be about fostering a real love of learning, and exploring beyond the confines of the curriculum. Just for fun.

But the reality is that most parents turn to a tutor because their child is struggling. They want results. They want a quick fix. And sometimes, private tuition can provide it.

If it's one particular topic or area that's a problem, then even just a one-off session can be enough to clear things up. And that's fine. But you also have to be realistic. If your child is predicted a D grade in English GCSE, and then a fortnight before the exam you call in a tutor, well, there's no way on earth they'll be able to turn that D into an A or B grade. Give them two years, and they might be able to do it. Two weeks? No chance. I once did some tutoring in my spare time, but I was very careful about who I took on. It wasn't the children that were the problem – it was the parents. Too many had unrealistic expectations and seemed to think a tutor could turn things round overnight. But if a child is struggling, there are usually complex reasons that take time to resolve. I even had one anxious mum ring up and ask if I could 'help' with her son's coursework. She'd pay me whatever I wanted. It soon became clear that she was really asking if I would do the coursework for him. The answer, of course, was no.

So before turning to tutors, think carefully about why you're doing it, and what you hope it will achieve. If you and your child are clear about what you want from a tutor, there's a better chance that things will work out.

CHOOSING A TUTOR

Want to become a personal tutor? Well, go ahead. All you have to do is stick an advert in the local paper. You might have no qualifications, no teaching experience, and no idea about the GCSE syllabus. But that doesn't stop you advertising your services. Chances are you'll even get a few customers, though you might not keep them very long.

Finding a tutor is easy. There are thousands of them, up and down the country. At one time you had to rely on scanning the small ads in the greengrocer's window. Now there are national tutoring agencies, often with more than 10,000 teachers on their books. But there's a difference between finding any old tutor and finding a good tutor. That's much harder. The private-tuition industry isn't regulated, so you need to be cautious. Going through a tutoring agency is an obvious first move. In theory, they should be trying to protect their reputation by only employing decent tutors. They should be able to put you in touch with someone who specialises in the right area for your child. And they will also run criminal-record checks on tutors, to make sure they're not barred from working with children.

But don't assume that a tutor must be wonderful, just because they belong to an agency called Wonderful Tutors. In reality, many agencies have no idea about the quality of the tutors on their books. They've never seen them work. They just have a list of names on a computer screen. They put you in touch with someone and claim their 10 per cent fee back from the tutor. It's better by far to find a tutor through word of mouth. So ask around, and try to get a personal recommendation.

When you do find the name of a tutor, always ask to meet them in person before agreeing to employ them. And when you do meet them, don't be afraid to ask about the nitty-gritty. Where and when did they study? How do they keep up to date with syllabuses? What do they think they can do for your child? How flexible are they about arrangements? How much will they charge?

Ideally, a tutor should be well qualified. It's more important that they know their stuff than that they have classroom experience. After all, being able to control a class of thirty isn't relevant when it comes to private tuition. But they do need to be up to date with what is being taught in school. There's nothing worse than your child being told things by their tutor that contradict what their regular teacher is saying. It just leads to confusion. And if the tutoring is aimed at improving SATs or GCSE results then you need to make sure the tutor knows the syllabus. If they don't, the sessions probably won't be much use.

In general, it's probably best to either use a current teacher, who's doing a bit of one-to-one teaching to earn extra cash, or a full-time tutor, who makes a living from their private work and treats it like a business. Be wary of those who just dabble.

Then there are the practical arrangements to consider. At home or away? Some tutors expect you to bring your child to their house. Others are willing to travel. In general, it usually works better if the lessons take place at the tutor's home. Children tend to respond to the idea of sessions being programmed and orderly, rather than an interruption to free time at home, and sometimes they get uncomfortable if they feel that parents are hovering in the background, keeping an eye on them.

Some tutors charge much more than others. An experienced tutor in the London area, with a reputation for getting children into fiercely selective schools, may charge £50 a lesson. A student trying to pay off their overdraft might settle for a tenner. Some tutors charge extra for marking and preparation, while others include that fee in their hourly rate. It's the quality of the teaching that counts. If you don't think you're getting value for money, then change.

Next Steps

- The Association of Tutors (www.tutor.co.uk) is the national body for private tutors. It publishes booklets and provides information for both parents and tutors.
- There are dozens of tutoring agencies across the UK: a quick search on the Internet should show up the ones in your area. Educational consultants Gabbitas (www.gabbitas.co.uk) offer parents independent advice on finding the best tutor. There is a £40 introduction fee.

If you think your child would really benefit from some extra coaching, but you can't afford the money, then you could consider grouping together with other parents and splitting the cost. There's not much difference between a private lesson for one, and a private lesson for three or four. They both guarantee lots of attention and a relaxed, positive atmosphere. There's also a growing market in online tuition. One company offers lessons over the Internet, with qualified tutors based in India, in one-hour sessions, day and night. Children can communicate by headphones and microphone, and work through exercises on their computer screens. It's not ideal, and it lacks the personal touch, but it may still be better than nothing if money is tight.

Finally, don't forget to check what's on offer at your child's school. It may have conveniently slipped his mind to tell you. Or he may not even know himself. But many schools now run out-of-hours support classes, especially when exams are coming up. They're free of charge, and the teachers will already know where your child's weaknesses lie. Some schools will even pay for a private tutor if, for example, they think a child is a borderline C or D grade at GCSE. After all, the school wants its results and statistics to be as good as possible.

Things To Do

- If you think your child might benefit from some one-to-one coaching, talk it through with them. If they're struggling in a particular subject, talk about the reasons.
- Discuss the idea of a tutor with your child's teacher. They'll give you their own opinion on whether it might be useful. Some teachers might be sensitive about their pupils getting extra help, and see it as a slur on their teaching abilities. But good teachers will be happy to advise, and may even be able to recommend a tutor.

HOME-SCHOOLING

This book is about helping your child to succeed at school. It's about how you can support the work that teachers do, and consolidate the learning that goes on in the classroom. So perhaps it's surprising to devote a part of it to the idea of not actually sending your child to school at all.

Home education isn't common. It's still seen as slightly strange. But there are signs that attitudes may be starting to shift. Every year the number of children educated at home grows by the equivalent of a large comprehensive. So it's worth just pausing to consider what home education is, and why more and more people are giving it a try.

There's some evidence that home-schooled children make quicker progress than those in schools. That's probably not surprising, as they can move at their own pace. And many of them work steadily all through the year, rather than doing lots in term time and nothing in the holidays. One study in the US suggested that home-educated children are usually around two years ahead of their classroom-based friends. Research in the UK shows that 82 per cent of home-educated children are in the top band for literacy at the age of ten, compared to a national average of just 16 per cent. And, of course, from time to time there are stories of a home-educated 'child genius' who sits his A levels early and gets a place at university when most kids are sitting GCSEs. But that kind of hothousing isn't always healthy – and probably isn't a fair representation of what home education is really about.

The practicalities

Education is compulsory. School is not. If you want to withdraw your child from school, all you need do is write a note to the head teacher. But if you do opt out, you're legally obliged to provide your child with an alternative form of school. In the UK about 1 per cent of children are educated at home, but the figure is edging upwards. There's a growing interest in the idea of personalised education, and what could be more personal than having your own school.

But is home education something you should think about seriously? Like any other form of DIY, it depends on your level of skill. You wouldn't think about rewiring your house if you knew nothing about electrics. And you shouldn't think about taking charge of your child's schooling if you know nothing about education. Having said that, it's important to get away from the idea that home-schooled children spend all day sitting around the kitchen table being taught maths by their mum. Home education is about more than an extension of do-good parenting: the point of it is that it encourages children to be independent. They learn how to research things for themselves, rather than being spoon-fed by a teacher. They have the freedom to follow their interests and passions, instead of following the curriculum. They can be guided by instinct, not by the school bell. If you stop to think about it, putting thirty children in a small room, day after day, is slightly odd. Making them all learn the same things is even odder. You might even compare regular school to battery-farming, and see home education as a free-range alternative.

So no, children don't take notes while their parents drone on about photosynthesis. And they don't just sit there working their way through the same textbook they'd be working their way through in school. If home education is just a school in a kitchen, then what's the point? Instead, home-schoolers learn in a variety of ways. They carry out research using libraries and the Internet. They have outings to museums and galleries. They may spend part of the week in small groups with other home-schooled children, which allows them to do activities such as drama or music. And they often belong to sports clubs or dance groups, which means they get plenty of social contact. Many parents also employ a handful of personal tutors, to provide specialist teaching and to help prepare children for exams. But the point is, it's flexible. Most home-schooling is very informal, with children simply given time to explore their own ideas and interests in whatever way suits them best.

That might sound like a recipe for disaster, especially if a child is lazy and disinterested. And it's true that home-schooling won't suit every child, just as regular schooling doesn't suit every child. But there are plenty of checks in place to make sure home-schooling is not just a euphemism for neglecting education altogether. The local education authority often visits families who home-school, and asks to see evidence that the children are learning and not just being left to their own devices all day. If they're not happy, they can seek a court order and have the child sent back to school. But it's extremely rare for that to happen.

Did You Know?

- One in four home educators is a teacher.
- Parents who choose never to send their children to school do not have to tell anyone of their decision.
- There were twenty families home-educating in the UK twenty years ago; now there are more than 30,000.
- In the United States, 5 per cent of children – 1.3 million – are educated at home.
- Home-educated children perform well above average in national literacy tests. Far less is known about how they fare at GCSE, A level and university.

It's estimated that over 100,000 children are educated at home in the UK. But it's hard to be exact, because parents who never send their children to school don't have to tell anyone. In other countries things are different. Some take a hard line: in Germany, for example, it's illegal to educate a child at home. Others have a long-established system of home-schooling that is much more popular than in the UK. In the US, around 5 per cent of young people are educated at home full time, while many more spend part of the week in school, and part of the week studying at home. It's a sort of mix-and-match education that allows children to follow their interests, but gives them the social structure of school to fall back on when they need help. There's nothing to stop you doing something similar in the UK, but you have to get your child's school to agree to it. Otherwise, it's truancy.

Some educationists think that home education will really take off in the next twenty years. They argue that schools of the future – particularly secondary schools – will be much more flexible. Teachers will operate as personal tutors, overseeing the progress of a number of children, lessons will be delivered by computer, and schools will become community resource centres, where children 'drop by' as and when they want. Time will tell.

Good for some, not for others

Under what circumstances should you consider home education? It's a difficult question. Many parents who take their child out of school do so because they don't like the situation at a particular school. There may be a problem with discipline, for example, and they think their child isn't making progress. Or their child may be getting bullied. Or there may be an argument with the school over uniform or behaviour. These parents don't actually *want* to educate their child at home. They see it as the last resort. They feel forced into it. And that's not a sound basis for making such an important decision.

Choosing to home-educate should always be a positive decision. You should do it because you genuinely believe that your child will flourish that way. I know the head teacher of one independent school – an excellent school, with a fine reputation – whose daughter was home-educated because he felt that it was right for her. And more importantly, she felt the same way. She learned at home between the ages of five and ten and loved it. It gave her time to learn musical instruments and play lots of sports. It meant she could establish a wide range of interests. At the age of eleven she went to school, because she wanted to. She did very well in her exams and won a place at Cambridge. Home education worked for her when she was young. School worked for her when she was older. My advice is simple. If you don't like your child's school, then change school. Only home-educate if you really think it's the right thing to do – if you find it an exciting idea. And remember that there's a great deal of sacrifice and hard work involved, with one or both parents having to be at home during the day to supervise. And you'll have to foot the bill for books and resources.

If it still appeals, then where do you start? The first step is to talk it through with your child. If you choose to take him out of school, then you're making him 'different'. And lots of children don't want to be different. You have to see things from his point of view. For many children, school offers a supportive and protective environment, where they can be with their friends. Before you go imposing your own ideas and ideals, you need to get his side of the story.

The next step is to make contact with other parents who are in the same boat. There's a growing network of home-educators who share ideas and resources. Taking your child out of school is a big decision, and you'll probably be grateful for a guiding hand from others who've gone down the same route. Depending on the age of your child, you'll also need to decide whether or not he's going to be taking exams. Missing out on SATs is no big deal, but GCSE and A-level qualifications can be important. It's perfectly possible for home-educated children to take exams, but they'll probably need to go into a local school or college to actually sit the paper. So you need to make arrangements with the exam board well in advance.

You also need to give careful thought as to how your child will make friends. Children need a social life. If they go to school, then that's probably where they will make most of their friends. If they don't go to school then it's harder work, but not impossible. It will probably mean taking up hobbies, playing sport or joining clubs.

Finally, you should always remember that taking your child out of school is not an irreversible decision. If you're planning to give home education a go, you can try it for six months or a year and see how it pans out. If it's not working, then don't be afraid to admit your mistake.

Next Steps

If you want to find out more about home education, you could try one of the following websites:

www.education-otherwise.org

www.home-education.org.uk

www.heas.org.uk

Part III

SMART LEARNING

9. LAYING THE GROUNDWORK: THE BUILDING BLOCKS OF YOUR CHILD'S EDUCATION

Fiona's new baby is lovely. She's eating and sleeping well and keeping her parents royally entertained. She's also starting to learn. She's begun her education.

From the moment your child is born, learning has started. Some of it will happen naturally. Some of it will need teaching. All of it will benefit from your knowledge and guidance. Get the basics right, and the rest will follow.

PLAY

It's not a mistake. Play is as much a part of your child's education as maths homework and a trip to the local museum. And because children start playing from such an early age, it's an important foundation for lots of the more structured work that comes later. Children learn through play. One study in the US found that children who played very little had lower IQs than their more playful classmates. Which shouldn't be all that surprising. Play is how toddlers discover the world and themselves. It's how older children develop their skills.

Play is something that comes naturally to most children. You don't need to spend lots of money on fancy toys. We've all seen children receive expensive presents, and end up being more interested in the cardboard they came packaged in. Generally speaking, a small selection of different toys is enough. Your child's imagination will make the most of them. When your child loses interest or grows out of a toy, then it's time to replace it. But some toys may remain favourites for years. And a bulging box of toys should never be a substitute for spending time with your child. Many children are happier spending time with their parents than being left alone with their toys, and children often enjoy helping out with 'adult' activities like gardening or cooking.

Don't be pushy when it comes to telling your child how to play. The whole point of play is that it's about freedom. A well-balanced child will spend some time playing physically, and some time playing mentally. She will spend time with friends, and she will spend time alone. If your child only shows interest in one kind of play, then you may need to guide her towards different activities. But tread softly. There are lots of games and toys that claim to have educational value. They may improve certain skills or encourage children to think. And that's great. But play time belongs to your child. Don't insist she uses a particular toy or game, if all she wants to do is throw a bouncy ball against a wall.

Play is always healthy and beneficial, even if it just allows children to switch off and relax. If your child wants to play a word or number game with you, then great. But there will be times when she just wants something unchallenging – and that's fine too. Finally, try to encourage your child to bring a sense of play to her schoolwork. Lots of schoolwork is great fun: writing stories, painting pictures, solving puzzles, researching new topics. These things aren't work. They're play. And if you can help your child see that work and play aren't always separate things, it will help promote a positive approach to learning.

If you're going to make one suggestion to your child, then maybe it should be that she learns to play a musical instrument. There's some evidence that playing music may boost some mental functions and improve concentration. In musicians, the parts of the brain concerned with movement and co-ordination tend to be bigger than in most non-musicians. And one study of pre-school children who were given piano lessons found they did better than other children when set problems and maths puzzles. The evidence isn't conclusive, but it's an area that's being actively researched. And since learning a musical instrument is also great fun, it's something that you should definitely encourage. There's even a suggestion that just listening to music can make us smarter, at least temporarily – the 'Mozart Effect', as it's sometimes known. In one study, children who listened to classical music before taking a spatial-reasoning test fared better than those who didn't.

But what about all those activities that some people claim stunt children's development, like watching TV or playing video games? Well, as part of a balanced programme of play, they're fine. In fact, they're positively beneficial. Watching TV can make children cleverer. Young people today are often sharp, witty and sophisticated. They are certainly much more media-aware than the teenagers of twenty or even ten years ago. They can watch sophisticated comedies and appreciate characterisation and irony. They can watch advertisements and see through the hard sell. They can watch films with complex narratives involving flashbacks or flash-forwards. In short, they are TV-literate.

But there's a balance to be struck. TV can stimulate children's curiosity. It can fire up a passion for sport, travel or science.

But for all its good points, watching TV isn't an active pastime. Nor is it an interactive pastime. A minority of children spend too much time watching wall-to-wall TV, regardless of whether or not they're really interested in what's on the screen in front of them. Your child *can* learn from TV, but she also needs the skills she learns from physical play, from exploring, from making, from socialising. If her addiction to TV has begun to shut these other things out, then it's gone too far.

The Internet is generally a more interactive medium than TV: it involves children in reading and responding to what they see on the screen. Of course, there's plenty of dross on the web. There's crazy stuff: pornography, advice on how to make explosives, and so on. But don't be afraid. For better or worse, the Internet reflects what the world is really like. And the world is a fairly mad place. With younger children you'll probably want to use a filter that blocks some of the less desirable material. But as your child gets older, it's best to put an end to the censorship and just let them explore. Teaching your child how to use search engines and how to make the most of the web is one of the most important things you can do. It's a fabulous resource.

Video games can be great too. There are challenging quest-style games, that require problem-solving, creativity and good memory skills. There are shooting, racing and fighting games that require hand-eye co-ordination, spatial awareness, and a keen sense of strategy. In fact, very few video games could be described as 'mindless'. They nearly all engage the brain in some way or other. And they teach children how to work towards targets and handle frustrations.

With TV, video games and the Internet it's a question of common sense, a question of control. Quality control. Time control. Self-control. In moderation, video games are a good thing. Some TV programmes are excellent. And watching a good film can be every bit as thought-provoking and stimulating as a trip to the theatre.

It's up to you to judge how much is too much. But rather

than laying down the law and saying, 'No more than an hour a day', why not try a different tack. Don't say, 'I think you've been watching too much television.' Instead say, 'Let's go ten-pin bowling tonight!' Be positive. If your child enjoys a range of activities, then she'll share her time between them. But it's up to you to encourage her interests, and to make it easy for your child to do different things. Maybe she would rather be out playing with her friends, but it would mean asking you for a lift. If that's the case then you need to be approachable and available. If your child seems to spend too much time on a games console or watching TV, then think carefully about whether you're offering any real alternatives. If you're not willing to engage with your child and make time for her, then it's only natural that she's going to switch on the one thing that's always there for her – the TV.

FIRST WORDS

Believe it or not, some parents don't really talk to their children. They ga-ga baby sounds at them when they're little; they throw occasional orders their way and they get through the business of life: 'What do you want for tea?' – 'Take your shoes off' – 'Time for bed'. But they don't really *talk*. They don't help their child explore language; they don't play with sounds; they don't show what words can do.

Even then, a child will still learn to speak fine. The ability to learn language seems to be a natural human instinct. The babbling of a baby has many more sounds in it than she will need when she eventually starts talking. And she has an amazing ability to pick up and process the sounds around her. Unless deprived of all stimulation, almost every child learns to speak their native language.

But you can do so much more. Most of the time we communicate with other people by speaking. We interact with other people by talking and listening. It's our verbal communication skills that shape our identity, that give us confidence, and help us strike up friendships. They lay the basis for other important language skills, like reading and writing, and they enable us to explore and express what we are learning.

So from an early age you need to make sure your child is talking and listening, *and* that she's talked to and listened to. Don't worry obsessively about how fast she's developing. Just talk to her. Read to her. Sing to her. Recite rhymes and poetry. And when she talks to you, engage with her. Answer her. Encourage her.

It sounds obvious, and it is. But there are so many other things competing for our attention – televisions, computers, mobile phones – that children don't always get our full attention. Speaking to your child and encouraging her to talk is one of the most important things you can do. You should make it a priority.

Did You Know?

- 74 per cent of head teachers in the UK say they are concerned by the numbers of children who arrive at school with poorly developed speaking and listening skills.
- In many European countries – including Finland and Sweden – emphasis in the early years is on speaking and listening. Children may not be taught to read until the age of seven. These countries have excellent rates of literacy.

READING

Learning to speak is the first step towards learning to read. If a child is well grounded in spoken language, she will find it much easier when she starts reading. Reading is not like speaking: it doesn't come naturally. It has to be taught. In many ways, it's like learning a code. Children need to make the connection between what they see on the page, the sounds they hear and the meanings attached to words. Do that and they've cracked it!

When it comes to teaching children to read there are two frequent responses from parents. There are those who are wary of getting involved and who prefer to leave it to the professionals at school. Then there are those who are anxious that their children should start to read as early as possible so they can be 'ahead' of others in their class. Neither approach is very helpful.

There are lots of simple things you can do to help your child learn to read. There's certainly no need to feel daunted. The important thing is not to push her before she's ready and to make sure you work closely with the school. That means finding out more about how your child will be taught to read – because different schools have different approaches.

Some schools use a sound-based system known as phonics. Teaching children to read using phonics means breaking down each word into individual units of sound. The most methodical system is known as synthetic phonics – where words are broken down as far as they will go. So the word 'street' would be split into five units: s-t-r-ee-t. There's another system, known as analytic phonics, which breaks words down, but not quite so rigorously. So street might only be broken into two units: str-eet. Most schools now favour the synthetic phonics approach. It seems to be the best method for children who have difficulty learning to read, such as dyslexics. You can recognise reading books for children who are learning phonics because they tend to focus on a single sound, or letter, repeated over and over.

Other schools think phonics is a rather dull way of teaching something as rich and wonderful as language. They prefer to use a visual approach, usually called 'whole language', which teaches children to recognise whole words. Many children, for example, first learn to read by recognising their name. They grow familiar with the shape of the word. They know what it sounds like. And eventually they put two and two together. The 'whole word' or 'whole language' approach usually involves children reading plenty of different books and working out what words mean from the context around them. It's a more adventurous approach, which suits good readers. Children pick things up as they go along, and remember how different words are written and pronounced. Reading books for children learning this way usually have a normal range of different words and sounds.

So which reading method is best? Well, the jury's still out on that one. Looking at the latest research, they'd probably come down in favour of phonics. But it wouldn't be unanimous.

Of course, it's possible to mix and match the two methods. In some ways that's what happens naturally. Children who are taught phonics soon become 'real' readers. Children who are taught to recognise whole words can't help but pick up the phonemic rules. It's important to know how your child is being taught because it makes sense to reinforce the work that's being done in school. But that doesn't mean you have to do exactly the same thing. If your child is learning through phonics, maybe you could try encouraging them to 'say and see' whole words. You could write fifty simple words in large letters on pieces of card, and teach your child how each word is said, then get them to repeat the word. But if there's a problem, then break the word down. Fall back on the approach your child is most familiar with.

Things To Do

- If your child is stuck for reading ideas then a teacher should be able to provide a recommended reading list for different age groups. Or speak to a librarian. But there's nothing more satisfying than seeing your child browsing the shelves of a bookshop, and picking out something for herself.

- Try reading the same books as your child. Not all the time – just every now and then. It will help you to get some idea of what she enjoys reading and may also lead to some interesting discussions.
- Books don't just have to be read. Talking books can be really useful for car journeys, or if your child likes to listen to something before she goes to sleep.

Learning the mechanics of reading is only the start of it. If you want your child to develop a genuine love of reading, then you need to encourage her right through the school years. When she's still young, you can read to her and get her to read short passages to you. Read stories together, out loud, taking turns. As she gets older, it's more a question of making sure that she has the right books and materials – things that really grab her interest. Don't have a fixed idea of what she should or shouldn't be reading. It might be comics, magazines or newspapers. Or she might prefer reading online, rather than a printed book. If she has a particular interest, like sport, then she may want books about that subject. Don't worry too much about *what* your child is reading. The important thing is that they *are* reading. If children read regularly, then they'll learn to love it. And they will naturally start to branch out, and to choose more adventurous or demanding books.

There's nothing more likely to discourage your child than insisting she reads things she doesn't like. By all means suggest ideas, and there's no harm in buying books you think she might enjoy. But don't pressure her to read a particular book just because you think it would be good for her.

STRUGGLING TO READ AND DYSLEXIA

Dyslexia comes from the Greek, meaning 'difficulty with words'. And even though scientists have been researching the subject left, right and centre for the last twenty years, that literal translation is still the best definition of what dyslexia is – difficulty with words. Because despite all the money and time spent on research, there's still no consensus about what causes dyslexia, and what the exact signs of dyslexia are.

Lots of children find reading difficult. Are they all dyslexics? Some would say no. They argue that dyslexia is a genetic and partly hereditary condition. They believe that the brains of dyslexic children process information differently. In dyslexic people, the connections between different language areas of the brain do not work as efficiently as they should. The brain cells themselves may even be structured differently. Dyslexia is something you either have or you don't.

A different view is that dyslexia is simply the label we give to those at the bottom end of the reading scale. It's a catch-all term, that groups together children who may have very different difficulties.

For some children, being called dyslexic just makes their problems worse. It demoralises them and lowers their expectations. Other children like the idea that there is an explanation for their difficulties. It comes as a relief. 'At least I'm not stupid,' they think. In many ways, only two things really matter. The first is that children's reading difficulties get picked up (and the sooner, the better). The second is that they are then given appropriate help, which allows them to overcome those difficulties. And one advantage to children being assessed and termed dyslexic is that it entitles them to extra help and support, which they otherwise might not get.

The ability to read well doesn't seem to be closely connected to intelligence. Among children who struggle with their reading, there are people with high IQs, low IQs and average IQs. Most children who struggle with reading and writing do so because they have problems processing the sounds of the language. They have difficulty linking what they hear to the letters they see on the page. In countries where the link between sounds and spellings is straightforward, relatively few children are classed as dyslexic. In countries where the language contains lots of irregular spellings, rates of dyslexia are much higher. The bad news is that the English language is a nightmare. Hundreds of words are spelled irregularly or just plain illogically.

With very young children, it may be possible to spot the warning signs even before they begin to read and write. Dyslexia is often linked to problems with the short-term memory, or with difficulty in remembering sequences. So when she recites the days of the week, or counts to ten, a dyslexic child may get the order wrong. She may jumble up letters in her words, use the wrong words for simple objects, or cobble together new words from different parts of other words. All young children do these things – it's part of the learning process. But if it seems unusually persistent, then it may be a sign that she isn't finding it easy to process the sounds she hears.

When children do begin to read and write, signs of possible dyslexia include getting letters the wrong way round within words, or missing out letters altogether. Or confusing similar-sounding letters, both when reading or writing, such as b and d, or s and z. Other signs to look out for are writing very slowly and untidily, or taking ages to complete homework. Difficulty with general organisation, such as remembering things that need to be done or putting clothes on back to front, can also be a sign of possible dyslexia. And if your child is getting exceptionally tired, that may also be a telltale sign: dyslexics can often find the school day exhausting if they have to do a lot of reading and writing.

Dyslexia isn't a disease. There's no 'cure', as such. But with hard work and the right support, most dyslexic children are able to make good progress.

Schools are usually quick to pick up on the signs of dyslexia. There are lots of different tests they can give to children, designed to highlight any problems that are out of the ordinary. One of the problems, though, is that there is no one standard test, used in all schools.

It's easier to help children if their difficulties are picked up at an early age. But that's the time when it's hardest to spot those difficulties. After all, when children are just starting to learn, they all make lots of mistakes. So children with particular difficulties don't always stand out. And inevitably, some teachers are better than others at identifying potential strugglers.

If you worry that your child may have dyslexia that hasn't been picked up on, it's best to speak to her class teacher. If you're still concerned, then you should ask to see the school's Special Educational Needs co-ordinator. You could also consider having a private assessment of your child carried out by an independent education psychologist. And the British Dyslexia Association is able to put parents in touch with local support groups who can offer advice.

There's also the possibility of employing a private tutor who specialises in teaching children with reading difficulties, to support the work being done in school.

If your child seems to have been reading all right, but suddenly starts struggling, check out some practical things. Are the books simply too hard? Can she see the words properly, or does she need an eyesight test? Has she changed teacher recently? You need to make sure that your child's school has a structured approach to teaching reading and writing. That means every teacher in the school should teach literacy in the same way, so that children don't get confused when they change classes.

Still struggling? If the school has a 'whole word' approach to teaching reading, you should think carefully whether this is right for your child. Dyslexics and other poor readers benefit from a phonics-based approach. They should be taught the most frequently used ways of pronouncing different combinations of letters and then taught the alternatives. Where there are rules they should learn them. Where there are exceptions they should learn them. A pick-it-up-as-you-go-along approach just won't work. New ideas need to be introduced gradually, and there should be lots of repetition and consolidation. There should also be good use of classroom assistants to allow the children to get one-to-one help as often as possible. Above all, dyslexic children seem to benefit from what's called a 'multi-sensory' approach. That means they look at words and practise saying them. They hear words and practise writing them. It may mean they spend time playing with models of words, shaping letters out of clay or Plasticine, or drawing letters on the floor in sand or chalk. Don't worry if this kind of approach seems unusual. It works.

If your child's school seems to tick all the boxes, then that's great. If not, don't be afraid to talk to the teacher and ask them about their methods. Good communication between you and the school is more important than ever if your child is dyslexic.

Did You Know?

- Dyslexia is the most common special educational need in the UK, affecting about 350,000 schoolchildren.
- There are 43 sounds in the English language – but hundreds of ways of spelling them.

It's important that dyslexic children improve their reading and writing skills. But it's also important that they engage with schoolwork in spite of their problems. That means making the learning process as easy as possible.

Technology can make a real difference. Is there a DVD or TV programme that covers the same ground as the textbook? Is the book they're studying available in audio form, on tape or CD? If note-taking in class is a problem, perhaps your child could record what the teacher says and play it back later. For those who find organisation a problem, there are electronic personal organisers. And making full use of a computer is very important. Children can run a spelling and grammar check over their work. And they can see what they've written clearly, and correct mistakes easily. It's a good idea to buy some touch-typing software that will teach them how to type quickly and efficiently. And encourage them to experiment with different fonts and different font sizes and colours. Some children will respond better to some typefaces than others. There are even talking word processors available. These say the words as they are typed, and many dyslexic children find them very helpful. Every month there are new advances – so try to keep up to date.

Do your best to help your child to read, but make sure she isn't defined by her dyslexia. It's just one small part of her. The most important thing of all is to make sure that no one labels her as stupid just because she's a poor reader or speller. If children who struggle with words are automatically shunted into the bottom set they will grow frustrated and dispirited. Dyslexic children often have exceptionally strong visual and spatial awareness. They may be very creative or particularly good at problem-solving. Plenty of famous people, such as Einstein and Rodin, are thought to have shown signs of dyslexia. And there are countless modern-day examples of people who have succeeded in different walks of life despite their dyslexia. Some people go so far as to say that dyslexia is a gift, which helps people see the world differently. So encourage your child to stay positive.

Things To Do

- Keep your child's confidence high, by focusing on her strengths. If she finds pictures and graphs easier than words and numbers, then encourage her to use them in her work whenever possible.
- Do lots of reading out loud with your child, even as she gets older. Make it fun. Never make it seem like homework or a chore. Even if she finds reading hard, she needs to stay enthusiastic about books.

- Don't wait for your child to be labelled dyslexic. If she's falling behind, then she needs extra help.
- As she gets older, encourage her to review written work carefully, checking and proofreading everything.

WRITING

When it comes to handwriting, parents face the same problem as with reading. Should they get their child off and running before they start school – or is it best to wait? But whereas you're unlikely to do much harm by teaching your child to read, when it comes to writing you need to know what you're doing. It's a technical business. Children need the right grip on the pen, and they need to learn to shape their letters correctly. Bad habits are easily learned, but difficult to shed.

Did You Know?

- Some countries, such as France and the US, have a national style of handwriting. In the UK, the decision rests with individual schools.
- Some schools teach joined-up writing in Year 1. Others wait until Year 3.
- Only one in three primary teachers claims to have received instruction in teaching handwriting during training.

As with reading, different schools teach writing in different ways. The most commonly taught style is known as semi-cursive, which is thought to be easy to learn, and easy to read. It encourages children to make rounded letter shapes and to join up most of the letters, but not all of them. But some schools still teach a fully cursive style, where the g's and y's have long loops that can join them to other letters. Either way, it's best if a school has a clear policy on the type of handwriting it teaches. Otherwise, your child may find one teacher telling her one thing, only for a different teacher to muddy the waters.

If children are going to learn how to write in a particular style, then that's the way they should start out. Assuming they are going to eventually join up their letters, then, right from the start, they should practise making letters with appropriate 'exit strokes'. If your child starts and ends letters in the correct places, then joining them up simply becomes a matter of moving from the end of one letter to the start of the next without lifting the pen.

But good schools will also allow children to develop their own individual style. If a child shows a natural tendency to write in italics, then that's fine – provided it isn't going to slow her down when she's writing against the clock in exams. Even writing that isn't joined up at all can be perfectly adequate. Done well, it looks neat and mature and some children manage to write very quickly in this printed style.

If you're going to teach your child to write then the most important thing is to make sure she holds the pen, pencil or crayon in the right way. Of all writing habits, that one is the hardest to change. The most widely used grip is known as the 'dynamic tripod', where the pen is held between the pad of the thumb and index finger, and rested on the middle finger. It's worth encouraging this grip even if your child is just scribbling or playing around with their crayons.

Things To Do

Whether or not you teach your child to write, or leave it to the school, there are plenty of other things you can encourage from an early age that will help when the time comes to learn handwriting:

- Get your child to practise drawing shapes, like circles and triangles.

- Encourage plenty of scribbling. Let your child make pictures outside with a wide range of different materials like chalk, paint or talcum powder.
- Tracing or doing 'join the dots' can help build up some of the motor skills needed for writing. It's even more fun if you let children draw with their fingers in piles of sand or shaving foam. Encourage them to make loops and zigzags, which will come in handy when they learn letter shapes.

SPELLING

Good reading and good spelling skills are closely connected. But most children have some problems with spellings, even if they read very well. That's because the English language is so chock-full of irregular spellings that just don't seem to make sense. Most children learn to spell simply through becoming familiar with what words look like, and learning the words they find tricky. And teachers will give them the rules that govern spelling, such as when to double up letters and when not to.

If your child still has problems with particular words, here are a few ideas. They can be used with children of any age.

- Copying out a word repeatedly may sound old-fashioned, but it can help the muscles in the hand 'remember' the correct spelling. It gives children a 'feel' for the word.
- Devising mnemonics is a good way of tackling the occasional word that children might trip up on. The word 'rhythm', for example, is a bit of a nightmare – unless you remember that Rhythm Helps Your Two Hips Move. The word 'necessary' also claims its share of victims, so remember that it's necessary to have one Coat and two Socks – one c and a double s. In fact, it shouldn't be a problem to make up your own mnemonics for whatever your child finds tricky.

- Encourage your child to take an interest in spelling by playing lots of word games like Scrabble or Boggle or hangman.
- Encourage your child to keep using words she finds difficult to spell, rather than just using a restricted vocabulary. She'll get there in the end.

MATHS

When children are asked which subject they find hardest at school there's one answer that always comes top – maths. But why do children find maths so tricky? Perhaps it's because so many parents are happy to help their children with reading, but not with maths. So make sure you spend as much time helping your child with her number skills as you do helping her develop her language skills.

It all comes down to attitude. Mathematical principles are behind many great inventions, like games consoles or iPods. But children still don't see maths as fun. It's up to you to make it interesting. And fortunately, maths lends itself to a whole range of games, activities and tricks. Think of a number; double it; add 4; multiply by 3; divide by 6; subtract 2. Don't tell me . . . you're back where you started. It seems like a fancy trick, but once children figure out why it works, they realise it's just a simple equation. In fact, introducing your child to the idea of equations is one of the most useful things you can do. When she learns that '3+4=7', for example, she needs to see that it is actually an equation, which is balanced on both sides. The question might be: '3+4=?' – or it might be '3+?=7'. It's the same question. If children understand this, then moving on to algebra shouldn't hold too many fears.

Japan regularly tops international numeracy tables, partly because it has such a strong tradition of playing number games. Sudoku may be about logic rather than arithmetic, but it gets children used to numbers and problem-solving. Kakuro is even better. Here in the UK, there are bundles of 'fun maths' resources in the shops. One favourite is a mathematical version of Scrabble, where children use a mixture of symbols and numbers to build equations, while everything from darts to dominoes and blackjack to bridge makes use of maths skills. So don't fall into the trap of getting your children into words and reading, while forgetting all about the numbers.

Did You Know?

Why do children often hate maths? One theory that has been suggested is that the part of the brain responsible for maths calculations may be closely connected to the part that registers anxiety. So feeling uneasy might make it more tricky to do sums, which in turn causes more anxiety – or 'maths panic'. The situation is probably made worse by the fact that early years maths tends to be about 'right or wrong' answers, with teachers often putting children on the spot by testing them on their tables.

DYSCALCULIA

Dyslexia has a mathematical equivalent known as dyscalculia. We know less about dyscalculia than about dyslexia – but it seems that a part of the brain connected with mathematical reasoning doesn't function in the usual way.

Dyscalculics may have problems with counting, or with sequences of numbers or telling the time. They may not be able to make simple associations, such as working out that '9+5' is the same thing as '5+9'. If you think your child really struggles with numbers then you should talk to their maths teacher. As with dyslexia, there are diagnostic tests that children can take. And it's important that teachers identify particular areas where a child struggles, because not all dyscalculics face the same problems.

Generally speaking, dyscalculics respond well to very active maths lessons, where they can move objects, beads or blocks. But they struggle when lessons are based just on talking, or on pen-and-paper calculations. And teachers should avoid asking dyscalculics to do sums on the spot in front of the class – it will just make them anxious and embarrassed.

Lots of dyslexic children also find maths tough going, but that doesn't necessarily mean they have dyscalculia. It may be that they have difficulty reading work on the whiteboard, or understanding the questions.

10. GETTING AHEAD: STUDY SKILLS THAT MAKE A DIFFERENCE

Sally is bright, but her teachers feel she's not making the most of her talents. She struggles to remember what she's learned in class, and she doesn't always shine in tests. They'd love to help more, but Sally is in a class with thirty other children. They simply don't have time.

To succeed at school, young people need to work well at home. They need to develop good note-taking and revision skills. And when exam time comes around, they need to remember what they've learned and get it all down on paper, before the clock runs out. It's a lot to ask. So let's look at the key study skills that can give your child an edge.

WORKING AT HOME

It's understandable if children aren't always enthusiastic about working outside of school. After all, there are plenty of adults who groan at the thought of taking work home after a long day at the office. But homework can be an important part of your child's education. It consolidates what's been learned in class, and lays the groundwork for future lessons. It allows teachers to assess progress, and encourages children to become independent learners.

If you want to encourage good home-study habits, then you need to make sure your house offers a suitable working environment. That doesn't just mean sticking a desk in your son's bedroom and letting him get on with it.

Different children work in different ways. Some will be happy with noise in the background, or with brothers and sisters buzzing round. Others prefer peace and quiet. Some children like a routine, others will work when the mood takes them.

The important thing is to talk to your child about how he likes to work. Don't make assumptions about what is best for them: you may think that listening to music is a distraction, but some people find it helps them to relax and concentrate. When it comes to studying it really is a case of each to their own.

But children also have to learn to be flexible. If they can only work under certain conditions, then they will run into problems when things aren't to their liking. My neighbour's daughter, Julie, used to prefer to do her homework in total silence. If she was working, no one else in her family dared make a sound. As she got older, so she became more and more sensitive to noise when she was trying to work. Her brother couldn't watch television, or practise his music. He couldn't have friends round. But then the time came for Julie to go off to university, to live in halls of residence with hundreds of other students, doing different courses at different times, coming and going, laughing and cooking and chatting. Julie found it impossible to work. When exam time came round at the end of her first year, she became so stressed that her parents had to hire her a country cottage for the week, so she could revise in peace!

Things To Do

Talk to your child about their learning preferences, and ask if there are changes you can make that might help them. It could be something as simple as changing a light bulb.

Find out when your child likes to work. Is it when he gets in from school, or later, after he's eaten? Try to establish a family routine that helps everyone to work at their preferred time.

Helping with homework

Helping with homework is a minefield.

Suppose your child is struggling with fractions. Do you give him encouragement? Give him a clue? Or just go ahead and give him the answer?

If you're only helping out because you want your child to get good marks, then think again. Homework is one way in which teachers can find out if topics covered in class have been fully understood. It helps them to identify those children who might need a little extra attention. If you end up doing most of the work yourself, then you may be glossing over problems. And that won't do your child any favours in the long term.

Did You Know?

According to a survey by the BBC:

- Parents of primary school children spend an average of six hours a week helping with homework.
- 53 per cent of parents help with homework every day.
- 69 per cent of parents say they would help more with homework if they were more confident in their own abilities.

No one likes to see their child struggling, but wrestling with a problem is actually an important part of cognitive development. If you want to get physically fit, you have to put in some hard work. No pain, no gain. Similarly, we only develop our mental capabilities by pushing and stretching ourselves; by working out what to do when we're stuck. If turning to Mum or Dad becomes the easy way out, then most children will take it. So don't rush to the rescue at the first sign of trouble.

There's one more question you need to ask yourself before you step in and help out – and it's an awkward one. Do you really know what you're talking about? If not, you're likely to do more harm than good. Bear in mind that things may have moved on since your day. Some primary schools now hold regular maths and English classes for parents, to introduce them to the latest teaching methods. It's a nice idea. But the reason they do this is because they're tired of parents who contradict what the teacher has been saying in class. They're right to be touchy about it: children need clarity, not confusion.

So, is it best to keep out of the way and let them get on with it? Not at all. You just need to show some good judgement.

There's nothing wrong with your child asking for help. In fact, it shows initiative. After all, using the resources around us, whether that means books, the Internet or other people, is a perfectly valid learning strategy. And there are plenty of ways for parents to help out, without doing all the work. Some children like to talk things through before getting started, so perhaps you could act as a sounding board for their ideas. If they're preparing for a test, you might be able to take on the role of quizmaster. You could also agree to look over finished work and offer suggestions for improvement.

The most important thing is to show an interest in your child's homework. And that means the work itself, not just the grades. Of course, you'll want to know about progress and results, but the more involved you are, the easier it is to ask how things are going. 'How did you get on with that piece about the Industrial Revolution?' sounds much more supportive than 'What mark did you get in history?'

Did You Know?

- The government issues guidelines to schools on the amount of homework children should receive.
- For primary school pupils, the recommended amount is an hour a week in Years 1 and 2, rising to two and a half hours a week in Years 5 and 6.
- For secondary school pupils, it's at least 45 minutes a day in Years 7 and 8, and up to two and a half hours a day in Years 10 and 11.

Primary schools often ask parents to sign a homework diary, to verify that work has been completed. But as children grow older most parents take a back seat. Teenagers like to be independent, and the work itself becomes more specialised, making it difficult for parents to get involved. But even if you can't offer advice about simultaneous equations or the periodic table, you may be able to help with other aspects, such as time management. Primary school homework usually has to be done for the next day's class, but older pupils can have much longer deadlines. It's a difficult adjustment, and a lot of teenagers need help organising their time. This could be anything from working out a to-do list to setting priorities or splitting big assignments into manageable daily chunks. The key is to sit down together, talk it through, and make it part of the homework process. That way it's less likely to look like nagging!

Did You Know?

- Helping with GCSE coursework is permitted under exam guidelines.
- Parents can discuss the coursework assignment with

their child, read and comment on drafts, and suggest possible sources of information. But they must not put pen to paper.

- 5 per cent of parents admit to writing part of their children's coursework.

If your child struggles with homework, or finds it hard to focus, it may be worth enquiring about homework clubs in your area. These are usually run by schools or libraries, and mean children can work in a structured environment, with a teacher on hand to offer help. Too often, homework can be a source of tension within the family. This kind of club can offer safe neutral ground and give everyone an hour or so of much-needed space. When I started out as a young teacher, I had the job of supervising the school library at the end of the day. One boy was in there every afternoon, doing his homework. At first, I assumed it was because his parents were unable to collect him at the right time, but it turned out he was there through choice. 'If I go home and work, my dad always interferes,' he explained. 'He tries to help, but he just gets in the way. We always fall out about it. It's much easier when he's not around.'

So by all means help out with homework, but try to be guided by your child. Show an interest in what he's doing, and let him know that if he needs assistance, he can ask for it. But encourage him to ask for specific help, instead of just saying, 'I'm stuck'. And if you think it would be better not to help, then be sure to give your reasons and to suggest a different way forwards. Maybe you could persuade him to ask a friend sometimes, instead of always turning to Mum or Dad? One of the big changes in schools over the last decade is that far more work is done in pairs or groups than used to be the case. It's not cheating, it's teamwork. And if you still have doubts about how much you should be helping out, then don't be afraid to discuss it with your child's teachers. They'll be happy to give you a few pointers.

Next Steps

To find out about homework clubs in your area visit your local authority website.

If you want to help out with homework but feel your sums are a bit rusty, get in touch with your local further education college. They often run courses for parents, with advice on how to help out with maths, science or English homework.

WORKING WITH YOUR MEMORY

A good memory is one of the cornerstones of success – at school and beyond. But today's children spend less time exercising their memories than their predecessors. Learning by rote was once an accepted part of school routine, but today the emphasis has shifted. Acquiring skills is the priority, not learning facts and figures by heart. And rightly so. Teach children how to search the Internet and they will have all the information they will ever need at their fingertips in a moment. Teach them to think critically and they will be able to analyse and interpret that information.

But a good memory remains a valuable asset. Most exams still require candidates to recall information, rather than research it. And the more that children can hold in their heads, the better equipped they will be to think on their feet and absorb new ideas.

Did You Know?

Some scientists believe that the human brain remembers everything that ever happens to us. We don't 'forget' anything, we just lose our ability to access those memories. This could explain why people who have near-death experiences often report seeing their whole life 'flash' before them.

Knowing how the memory works can help children train it to work better. It can save a lot of time that can be used for learning new things, and it can make the slog of exams less oppressive. A lot of children learn things at school, then forget about them until the test papers arrive. That might be days, weeks, or even months down the line. Suddenly, it's not so much a case of revising a topic, as relearning it from scratch.

For most people, this is not a very efficient way of working. It's much better to revisit what we've learned at frequent intervals. Experts believe that the brain stores information in two ways – in either our short- or long-term memories. By reviewing new information regularly, we can bring about its transfer from short-term to long-term storage. Whether it's a six-year-old learning their tables or a sixteen-year-old trying to remember the causes of World War I, the brain likes repetition. If children can review what they have learned at the end of each day, take another look at it the next day, again at the end of the week, and once more at the end of the month, then that information should be safely lodged in their long-term memory. It's not an easy way of working, but it is a very efficient way of working. If it becomes a habit, then when exams come around revision will be a simpler, less stressful process.

Things To Do

Encourage your child to talk to you about what they have done in school that day. It's one of the best ways of getting them to review what they've learned, and will help fix new information in their memories.

The memory also finds it easier to store information if it's given regular breaks, rather than overloaded with too much at once. It may help to think of the memory as a muscle, which gets tired if you use it for too long without a rest. So when trying to absorb new information, or revising for an exam, it's better to work in small blocks of time. Research suggests that the memory retains a greater amount of information just before a scheduled break, and again just afterwards. So by working in blocks of twenty to thirty minutes, the learning process will be more efficient.

Keeping calm and focused is also important, both when trying to absorb information, and when trying to recall it. We've all seen contestants on television quiz shows, who know the answer, but can't quite think of it. The pressure makes them 'go blank'. Many children face exactly the same problem when they are put on the spot by their teacher, or sat staring at an exam paper. Staying relaxed makes factual recall easier – but that's not always straightforward. Try to give your child confidence in their ability to remember, perhaps by playing memory games. Once they realise that their memory is reliable, at least most of the time, they should be able to relax.

Things To Do

There are lots of games you can play with your child that help develop memory skills. Here are some suggestions.

I went to market
The first player says, 'I went to market and I bought a chicken.' The next player repeats the sentence, but adds another item to the list. Each player must repeat all the items that have gone before, in the right order, then add one of their own. If you play regularly, you'll be surprised how quickly you improve.

Pairs of cards
Spread a pack of cards face down, arranged in rows. The first player turns over two cards. If they're a pair, they keep them and have another go. If they're not a pair, the cards are turned face down again, in the same place, and the next player takes their turn. By remembering where cards are positioned it becomes easier to find pairs.

Objects on a tray
Someone brings a tray of small objects into a room. Everyone looks at the objects for one minute before the tray is covered up or taken away. Players have to write down as many of the objects as they can remember.

Video games
Many computer games require good memory – particularly games of a 'quest' nature, where children have to remember what they learned from the last game in order to do better next time.

Memory systems

Scientists do not fully understand how the memory works. But one thing they agree on is that the human capacity to store information is far greater than most of us realise. Consider the feats of various world memory champions. There are people out there who can memorise the exact order of six packs of playing cards, recite whole novels word for word, or reel off the phone number of every Smith in the book.

So how do they do it? Well, memory experts have devised all kinds of systems designed to help their brains retain large amounts of information. Memory is closely linked to our senses. That's why a certain smell or particular song can trigger a memory we thought had long gone. Most memory systems rely on tapping into our senses and our imagination, in order to help us retrieve information. One of the simplest systems for remembering a long list of words is to come up with strong visual images related to each word, and then to form associations between each word and the next, perhaps by linking them together in a story.

Suppose your child has to remember four key words for a geography test: river, iron, motorway and farming. So he could imagine himself walking across a river of iron. On the other side of the river he meets a farmer. The farmer shows him a field where he is growing motorways. Growing motorways? It's a crazy idea. But the more unusual an image is, the more likely it is to stick in the memory.

This method works because the mind finds it easier to recall ideas that are linked together, and likes to remember visual images, rather than abstract words. And if the visual images can tap into other senses, then so much the better. Motorways? Think about the noise of lorries thundering down the M1. And if you need to remember the word 'soap', for example, don't just visualise any old piece of soap – imagine its colour, scent and feel. This kind of detail will fix the image in your memory.

Memory systems also explore the idea of 'pegging' the thing you want to remember to something that is already fixed in your memory. For example, some experts suggest thinking of a room you know well. If you have to remember ten words or facts, then you can place them in ten different places around the room. On top of the television, or on the coffee table. Under the bed. Up on the mantelpiece. In the cat basket. Then when you need to remember one of the facts, you just think of those 'pegs' and you will remember the thing you placed there. Again, it relies on imagination and association.

Memory systems tend to be geared up to learning long lists of words or numbers. That's great if you want to impress your friends, but it's not always easy to transfer these methods directly to the classroom, or to exam revision. Even so, they can be fun to play around with, and give a useful insight into how the memory works. In many ways, even the most complex system isn't so very different from a simple mnemonic, like the good old-fashioned Richard Of York Gave Battle In Vain. That phrase helps us to remember the colours of the rainbow, because the first letter of each word acts as a trigger. Memory systems don't work by magic: they just help to jog the memory.

Once children have some understanding of how the memory works, they'll be able to figure out their own ways of remembering things, and devise their own mnemonics. Let's suppose your child struggles to spell 'receive'. It's those three middle letters that are proving tricky. So what to do about it? He could write out the word twenty times. This has the advantage of repetition – which the memory likes – and it uses the body, which is good. When we write something several times, our hand begins to 'remember' how to write the word. It's the physical action that is being recalled. Or he could rely on that tried and trusted rule that makes use of simple rhyme: 'I before E except after C'. Or he could devise his own imaginative way of remembering: what about imagining *receiving* three presents, some Crayons, some Envelopes and some Ink? C . . . E . . . I. And if he makes the visualisation as vivid as possible – imagining the waxy feel of the crayons, the taste of the envelope on the tongue, and the black stain of ink on the fingers – then that will help to fix it in his mind.

NOTE-TAKING

Children spend a lot of time taking notes, and making notes. When they listen to teachers talk, when they're doing their own research, or when they're coming up with an essay plan that puts their thoughts into some kind of order – putting pen to paper is a big help.

But note-taking skills vary widely. Some children make random jottings, while others produce clear and well-organised annotations. When it comes to looking back over things, the quality of the notes can make a real difference. So how can your child improve his note-taking expertise?

One way is by learning how to 'map' thoughts and ideas. Mapping is a means of presenting information as a diagram rather than as a solid block of writing. At the centre of the diagram is the topic heading. Radiating outwards from that are the main subsections. Moving outwards again, there is further information related to each subsection. And so it goes on.

As a very simple example, a child could 'map' his family. At the centre he would write 'MY FAMILY'. Next, he might draw four lines heading out, north, south, east and west, leading to the words 'MUM', 'DAD', 'ME' and 'MY BROTHER'. Then from each of these there would be smaller lines, leading to other subsections, perhaps one for 'APPEARANCE', one for 'HOBBIES' and one for 'PERSONALITY'. Finally, another set of lines would radiate out from each of these subsections, leading to more detailed facts and information. You can use the same method to map the theme of guilt in *Macbeth*, or the causes of global warming. The basic approach doesn't change. It may help younger children to think of the map as a tree. The main idea is like the trunk of the tree, while the subheadings are like branches, which then have twigs and leaves attached to them.

Did You Know?

- The term 'mind-mapping' was coined in 1974 by learning guru Tony Buzan. But similar ways of organising information can be traced back to Ancient Greece.
- Mapping is thought to be of particular benefit to children with dyslexia.
- It's possible to buy mapping software packages that allow you to create maps on your computer.

Some people use the term mind-mapping, others use concept-mapping, thought-mapping, cognitive mapping or mind-modelling. Whatever you choose to call it, the idea is the same. It's about presenting information in a brain-friendly way.

So what makes mapping so good? Well, maps have lots of uses. They are an excellent way of note-taking, planning or revising. They group information in an ordered and uncluttered manner, which makes them simple to read and understand. They help children to organise their thoughts – and that's something young people often find difficult. They also force the mapper to be concise, and to think about what's really important. Perhaps most importantly of all, maps make it easier for children to remember information. That's because they show how one idea is linked to the next, so if you can remember the shape, structure and main headings of a map, that should give you the cues to recall the rest of the information. And because maps are easy to glance at when you've a spare moment or two, it means children can review the information regularly, which also helps them to remember it.

Mapping isn't complicated, but most people find it takes a little practice to really get the hang of things. The key to success is clarity. Start with a blank piece of paper – A4 is fine, but for a more complex map, you may need something bigger. Most people find that turning the paper on its side (landscape) works best. Write your key word, image or idea in the centre of the page. Then decide on your subheadings, and let the ideas flow from there. Remember that brevity is important. Limit yourself to key words, facts or phrases, rather than writing down whole sentences.

The more complex the subject you're mapping, the more layers of information you will need. A sophisticated map will also have lines that link different ideas together, even if they're not in the same subsection. So, if there's a link between an idea on the left side of the page and an idea on the right side of the page, you can draw a line between the two to make that clear.

Things To Do

There are no hard-and-fast rules to mapping. Encourage your child to play around, so they find a style that suits them. Possible ideas include:

- Using different colours.
- Writing in capital letters to make the map clear and memorable.
- Using pictures as well as words.

- Putting boxes around key points to help them stand out.
- Drawing two maps. One with plenty of detail, followed by a simpler version, or 'mini-map'.

Research carried out in 2002 found that university students who wrote down information in the form of a mind-map remembered 10 per cent more of what they had written than students who used other methods. But a word of warning. Some experts push forward great claims for mind-mapping. They say that mapping uses both the left and right sides of the brain, making children more creative and intelligent. They argue that other forms of note-taking are inferior and that mapping is always best. But not all children find mapping helpful. If your child has developed his own way of taking notes or organising his thoughts, then he may prefer to stick with that. By all means, encourage him to try mapping, but always remember that different children like to work in different ways.

Next Steps

Read about the impact of teaching mind-mapping techniques to a group of primary school children at: www.standards.dfes.gov.uk/ntrp/lib/pdf/Cain.pdf

WRITING FAST

It's not just mental skills that your child needs to hone. There's also an important physical skill that he needs to practise and develop. Handwriting.

Exams are designed to test intelligence, knowledge and understanding. And they do. But they also test the ability to write quickly. Some exams are multiple choice, but as children get older they are increasingly likely to have to write at length, particularly in subjects such as English or history.

Not surprisingly, children who can write quickly have an advantage here, and research in Oxfordshire secondary schools has shown a clear link between how fast children write and how well they fare at English GCSE. But schools rarely teach children how to write quickly. In fact, quite the reverse. Many teachers are obsessed with the need for neatness at all costs, even making children redo work that doesn't look nice and tidy. And parents take a similar approach, with proud mums and dads keen for their children to produce tidy, mature-looking work. It's like a kickback to the days of inky-faced Victorian clerks, when only someone with a perfect copperplate hand could get on. Handwriting is seen as an accomplishment; something to show off and admire. Quick, efficient handwriting, however, can be a tool for future success.

Did You Know?

- Only one in five schools has an active approach to speeding up children's writing.
- 40 per cent of girls and 25 per cent of boys of school leaving age complain of suffering pain when writing quickly.
- By the time children reach Year 11, some can write at over forty words a minute, compared to an average speed of just seventeen words a minute.

Some teachers will tell children that untidy handwriting will count against them in an exam, because it's likely to put the examiner in a bad mood. This simply isn't true. Examiners may have a tendency to grumpiness, but they are working to very strict marking schemes and unless work is genuinely illegible, it won't be marked down.

But if neatness doesn't matter, speed does: a failure to write quickly enough can, and does, cost marks. Ask children how they fared in an exam and one of the most common complaints is that they didn't 'get it all down'. And that's not just an excuse. If you walk into a school hall during the last half-hour of a GCSE or A-level exam, you'll see plenty of students flexing their fingers, hands and arms. They're struggling to write fast because they're not used to it.

You might think that children are either fast or slow writers, and that there's nothing you can do to change that. But often it's a case of practice and confidence. Regular 'training' sessions, against the clock, can make a real difference. Even just a few weeks of daily exercises should see a real improvement.

Things To Do

- Encourage your child to write as quickly as possible for two minutes. Giving them something to copy will mean they don't have to think what to write, and can concentrate on speed.
- Make it a daily exercise. With younger children you can turn it into a game, where they try to beat yesterday's score or set a personal best.
- Don't worry if their writing is a little bit messy, but if it becomes a real problem, try alternating – one day for speed, one day for neatness. That way your child will develop two styles of writing, a 'best hand' and a 'fast hand'. With time, the best hand will become quicker, and the fast hand neater, until they have attained a good all-purpose style of handwriting.

And if your child is still struggling, then try experimenting with different pens. When children learn to write they are taught a particular grip, which most will keep for the rest of their lives. But different grips suit different kinds of pen, and it may be that switching from, say, a ballpoint to a roller-ball, will improve both neatness and speed. It's even possible to buy pens designed especially for left-handers. Professional cricket players pick a bat to match their style; tennis players will have a favourite kind of racket; chefs choose knives that fit their hands: if a child is writing for hours and hours each day, it's worth trying to find a pen that suits.

As well as improving exam grades, learning to write quickly has plenty of other benefits. It can help with note-taking in class and make homework seem less of a chore. And it's not about improving the quantity, but also the quality of work. If children can write fluently, then there is less interruption to their train of thought, and ideas are more likely to flow.

So what about the computer revolution? Where does that leave pens, pencils and handwriting skills? There's little sign at the moment of schools allowing all their pupils to use word processors all of the time. But it's worth looking to the future if you want your child to get ahead. There may be a time when young people will have little need of handwriting, with almost all work, even exams, being word-processed. And even until then, there's still plenty of projects, assignments and homework that can be done on the computer. Yet schools are showing the same disregard for keyboard skills that they have shown for handwriting. While ICT lessons focus on computing know-how, very few children are taught how to type quickly and efficiently. They either pick it up, or they don't. Touch-typing is still seen as a secretarial skill, even though anyone who uses a computer keyboard would benefit from being able to type more quickly. If you really want your son or daughter to have a head start, then use the writing exercises outlined above for typing practice – and invest in some touch-typing classes.

11. STAYING ON TRACK: SOME OF THE THINGS THAT CAN GO WRONG

Amy used to like school. She used to be happy to set off in the mornings, and keen to tell her mum about her day. But recently she's refused to talk about her teachers, her classes or her friends. Her mum thinks it might just be that Amy's growing up. But there could be more to it, and she feels she needs to know.

Most children make it safely through their school career. They may have ups and downs, but in the end, things work out fine. Yet there are serious problems that can knock your child off track, and have ongoing repercussions for years to come. So it's worth knowing how to spot the telltale signs of trouble, and what to do when things go wrong.

BEING BULLIED

Being bullied can sour children's experience of school and disrupt their behaviour at home. It can damage their confidence and self-esteem. It can undermine, or even halt, their learning.

All schools have anti-bullying policies. It's a legal requirement. Some schools will even tell you they no longer have a problem. 'We don't have bullying here,' they say. But they're lying. Surveys suggest that more than half of all children experience bullying at some point during their time at school. In some cases it's an occasional incident in the playground, a fall-out with friends or a bad hair day. In other cases, it's sustained and brutal harassment over weeks, months or even years. Either way, the chances are that at some point during her schooling, your child will experience some level of bullying and will need the resources to deal with it.

The problem with bullying is that it happens in so many different ways and elicits so many different responses. Physical bullying can be terrifying, but at least it tends to be taken seriously by adults. There are the cuts and bruises to prove an attack, and teachers are unlikely to miss what's going on. Verbal bullying is more difficult to pin down, but can be extremely demoralising. The saying that 'sticks and stones may break your bones but words will never hurt you' is a load of old nonsense. Words can be extremely hurtful. Getting vicious texts on a mobile or hearing caustic insults thrown in the science lab can make a child feel isolated, vulnerable and desperately unhappy. Then there's emotional bullying, where an individual is excluded from a group or made to feel left out. This can be engineered in the most subtle and insidious of ways, and it can be almost impossible for a teacher or adult to see what's happening.

But if the problem is complex, it's also simple. Bullying is a problem because it makes children unhappy. And if you know that your child is unhappy, then you can take steps to deal with it. So if she tells you that she's being bullied, take her seriously. The very worst thing you can do is to shrug your shoulders and tell her not to worry about it. The reason she's told you is that she *is* worried. It may be a one-off incident. It may seem like nothing much. But it's your child's perception of it that matters, not yours. Many children who get bullied keep it to themselves. They may be embarrassed. They may think that the problem will just go away. They may feel there's no one they can confide in. So if your child comes to you and talks about it, that's taken a great deal of courage. You should be pleased. She trusts you. And she's taken a big step towards solving the problem. Assuming, of course, you respond in the right way.

So what should you do? Firstly, listen carefully to what your child has to say. Don't jump to conclusions. Not all cases of bullying are the same, and they can't all be handled in the same way. Encourage your child to give you as many details as possible. Try to find out what has happened, when it happened, and where it happened. Try to find out *why* it happened. When you've got all the information then you can consider what to do next. But don't go taking total charge of the situation. Keep talking it through with your child and asking her what she thinks the next move should be. She's in the thick of it; she's got a unique perspective.

Before you invest in a course of kick-boxing lessons, remember: encouraging your child to fight back – either verbally or physically – is rarely a good idea. It might work every now and then, but often it will make things worse. Bullies are looking for a reaction, so any kind of retaliation is just giving them something to feed off. And getting caught up in a cycle of playground violence is likely to end in some serious tears. Heading round to see the bully's parents is another sure way to inflame the situation, especially if you're feeling angry and protective. But the worst idea of all is to do nothing. It may be tempting to just hope the bullying stops of its own accord, or that the bullies move on to someone else.

But bullying needs to be nipped in the bud. If it goes unchecked, the situation is likely to get worse. The bully's confidence grows, while your child's self-esteem dwindles away.

So what options does that leave? Well, if the bullying is taking place in school, then you need to talk to a teacher. That probably means your child's form teacher first off, or perhaps someone more senior, such as the head or deputy. You need to give the school as much information as possible about the bullying, and you need to be clear and calm. Every child has a right to learn in a safe and supportive environment. You're not making a scene. You're not being overprotective. You're simply asserting your child's rights.

Situations like this need handling sensitively. Most children don't want teachers to know about bullying, because they worry that they'll be seen to be telling tales. Or they fear the bully might actually step up their harassment if they find out. But good teachers know this. They should be able to deal with the bully in a way that protects your child from any comeback. Find out what the school intends to do and don't be afraid to call back a few days later to make sure the matter's been dealt with. Always be supportive of the school's plan of action. But if it doesn't work, then ask them to try something else. If you're still not happy, then speak to a governor.

Telling the school about the bullying doesn't mean your job as a parent is over. You still have to support your child. Bullying can dent a child's confidence, and it's up to family and friends to rebuild that. You need to encourage your child to focus on the positive aspects of school. You need to help her understand that it isn't unusual to be bullied; it happens to most people at some point. Older children know this, but younger ones may think they're being singled out. And you should always encourage your child to be proud of who she is. If she's been bullied because she is in some way different to most of the children in school, then you need to take time to talk to them. Research shows that young people who are bullied most often think it has something to do with their appearance. Reassure your child that it's the bully who is in the wrong and who is acting abnormally. They are the one who has a problem.

It's also important that your child learns from her experiences. Most children are casual targets for bullies. They're picked on for no reason, other than being in the wrong place at the wrong time. But a small number of children seem to attract a queue of different bullies right through their years at school. So it's worth considering if there are things your child can do to stop herself becoming an easy target.

It's a balancing act. On the one hand it mustn't seem like you're blaming your child. Asking her if she did something to provoke the bullying, for example, might make it look like you're not on her side. At the same time, it's important to think about why your child has been bullied. Does she have a particular habit that other children don't like? Is it because she lacks confidence? Is it because she doesn't seem assertive enough, or because her body language makes her look vulnerable? Perhaps it's the opposite: she gets wound up easily and overreacts. Or maybe it's a practical thing. Perhaps she spends time in parts of the school where the bullies hang out. Or perhaps she needs to work on building up a network of friends, so as not to get isolated. Coming up with some kind of action plan is a good idea, because it helps children feel in control. It stops them feeling like a victim.

Because children often find it hard to admit that they're being bullied, it's important to be on the lookout for warning signs. Your child might stop talking to you about school or feign illness on certain days of the week. She might start coming home much later than normal, or take a long time at the end of the school day to calm down. Perhaps her results take a dip. Look out too for possessions going 'missing' more often than seems plausible. And in cases of physical bullying, there may well be cuts and bruises that tell their own story.

If you do have suspicions, then don't be afraid to ask your child outright if she's being bullied. She may well be looking for an opportunity to talk, and be relieved that you've raised it first. If she denies there's a problem, don't push it. Perhaps she's telling the truth. Perhaps she'll talk to you when she's ready. At least she will know that you're looking out for her, which should be reassuring.

DEALING WITH CYBER-BULLYING

Some parents draw on their own memories and experiences of childhood to help shape the way they deal with issues affecting their children. That can be helpful, but you also need to remember that schools have changed. Bullies have changed too. Cyber-bullying is a growing problem in many schools, with bullies harassing other children using the latest technology. That might mean bombarding their mobile phone with offensive text messages, or sending them aggressive emails. It might mean using computer photo software to create demeaning images, which are then sent round the school. Or using video phones to record incidents of bullying, which are then circulated among friends. In some cases, children have even set up 'hate websites' to make fun of another pupil.

Cyber-bullying can be very distressing. Technology makes it possible for the bullies to remain anonymous and abusive messages can be more hurtful if you don't know who's behind them. It makes it easier and quicker for nasty gossip to circulate, and something appearing in print on a computer screen can seem more momentous that a note scrawled on a scrap of paper. It's also possible for bullies to harass other children from a distance. Even in her own bedroom, your child could be targeted through their phone or computer. She can't just go home and shut the door on the bullies.

Dealing with cyber-bullying can be tricky. It's hard to prove anything, and many schools don't really understand the issues involved. They're much happier dealing with old-fashioned playground fisticuffs. But there are still some steps you can take to stop cyber-bullying getting out of hand. If your child tells you she's being bullied by text messages, don't over-react and take away her phone. That would be punishing your child, when she's done nothing wrong. Simply arrange for her to get a new mobile number, and tell her only to give it out to trusted friends. Most phone companies will change the number free of charge if you say it's because of harassment. Similarly, setting up a new email address is straightforward. And hate websites can be shut down if you can trace the company that is hosting the site. Your school's ICT teachers should be able to do this. It's also possible to trace which computer an email has been sent from and when it was sent. So, if the bullies are using the school computers it may be possible to catch them even if they're hiding behind a fake email. And if you do find out who's behind the messages, then Internet and mobile-phone providers have a duty to cut off their services, because repeatedly sending hate mail by phone or computer is a breach of the Telecommunications Act.

Things To Do

- Find an activity out of school that your child enjoys. If she's been physically bullied, then it may be that a martial arts class, such as judo or karate, will help instil confidence.
- Organise an outing for your child and a small group of her friends. It's important your child doesn't just withdraw from everything, or stop socialising.
- Try some role-play with your child, which gives her a chance to practise how to react in certain situations. Teach her to control her anger, by breathing deeply and counting to five before responding. Encourage her to ignore insults, rather than responding with one of her own. Show her how to be neither passive, nor aggressive – but instead to be assertive. That means making eye contact with the bully, and not being afraid to say no or to tell them to go away.

> ### Did You Know?
>
> - The children's charity ChildLine receives around 30,000 calls a year from bullied children.
> - Boys and girls are equally likely to be bullied, though boys have a higher chance of being attacked physically.
> - Every year, around fifteen young people commit suicide because of persistent bullying.
> - 14 per cent of children claim to have received abusive or threatening text messages on their mobile phone.

TRUANCY

As a parent, it's your responsibility to make sure your child goes to school. And it's not just a moral responsibility – it's a legal one. If your child regularly skips class, then you could be liable to prosecution, a hefty fine, or even imprisonment. That kind of scenario is rare – but truancy itself is worryingly common. Statistics show that around one in five secondary school pupils truant at least once a year – and on any given day there are tens of thousands of children who are out of school without permission.

Truants may not have permission, but they usually have their reasons. It might be that they just want to go to the shopping centre, but that kind of casual truancy is actually quite rare.

A far more likely cause of truancy is a bad relationship between the child and their teachers. Indeed, many truants don't skip whole days of school, they just stay away from a particular lesson where they don't get on with the teacher. And once that starts happening it's a vicious circle. The truant knows that turning up to the lesson means they risk being set extra work to catch up, or being made to look stupid because they aren't up to speed. So they're even more likely to truant.

If your child isn't getting on with a teacher then you need to step in before things break down completely. That may mean encouraging your child to forget past incidents and start afresh. But it might also mean talking to the teacher and asking them to show more understanding. It's all too common to have a situation where the teacher thinks a particular child has an 'attitude problem'. But often that bad attitude is the result of a child not feeling appreciated or respected by a teacher. And it's all too common for a pupil to think the teacher doesn't like them, when it's usually a case of the teacher feeling threatened or undermined in some way. Often it just needs a talk to clear the air – and it's sometimes parents who are best placed to act as peacemaker.

The two other common causes of truancy are bullying and boredom. Schools that work hard to clamp down on bullying have a lower rate of truancy, and so do schools that offer children alternative curriculum choices. If your son wants to become a car mechanic, then he may not see the point of studying history and French. And when teenagers don't see the point of something, they're quite likely to vote with their feet. In that case you need to talk it over with the school, to see if there's anything that can be done to make life more interesting and relevant. And try to help your child understand that truancy can be a slippery slope. Only 8 per cent of regular truants achieve five GCSEs, while truants are three times more likely than non-truants to commit a criminal offence. In fact, it's estimated that 5 per cent of all crime is carried out by truants when they should be at school.

Good schools work hard to combat truancy. They use electronic registration systems at the start of every lesson, not just first thing in the morning. If a child is absent, they call or text parents immediately. They organise regular patrols of remote corners of the school, where truants could be hiding out. They offer prizes for good attendance. But there's only so much schools can do – and they rely on parents to give them proper support.

Most parents are shocked if they find out their child has been playing truant. Yet the most common cause of unauthorised absence from school isn't children bunking off to play football.

It's mums and dads deciding to book family holidays during term time. In many ways, it's understandable. Flights and hotels are much cheaper outside of the school holidays, and you can save a lot of money. But you're also sending out the message that school isn't that important – at least not as important as the chance of a cheap holiday. That kind of attitude is bound to rub off on your child. If you take your child out of school then you're undermining the message that school comes first.

Did You Know?

- Every day, 55,000 pupils are out of school without permission.
- It's not just older kids who bunk off. A third of all truants begin skipping lessons at primary school.
- Truancy rates are roughly equal for boys and girls.

Things To Do

- Keep a check of how many days your child is absent from school through sickness each term. That way you can check if it tallies with the school's own records.
- Talk to your child regularly about what they do at school. Children are less likely to skip school if they think they will have to talk about what their day has been like. It makes it more likely they'll be found out.
- If your child seems to be doing badly in one particular subject, talk to them and find out if it's a problem with that teacher. If they're not seeing eye to eye then it needs sorting out straight away.

ALCOHOL

Binge drinking is a national phenomenon. The UK has the highest rates of underage alcohol consumption in Europe, and every year around 50,000 teenagers are admitted to hospital after drinking too much.

But is it just their health that's at risk, or can heavy drinking affect how children do at school? Of course it can. A national study of college students in the US found that D-grade students drank, on average, three times more alcohol than A-grade students. That's not to suggest that alcohol consumption was the only factor at work, or that D-grade students would suddenly start getting A's if they cut down on their drinking. But it does suggest that a lifestyle that involves plenty of drinking probably isn't conducive to hard or successful studying.

After heavy drinking, our learning capacity is reduced for up to three days. That is how long it takes the brain and the body to recover from the effects of dehydration and disturbed sleep patterns. There's even evidence that drinking can undo some of the learning done during the 24 hours before drinking, because it inhibits the transfer of knowledge from short- to long-term memory. And alcohol can also reduce the body's take-up of vitamins and minerals, so the brain may not get the supply of nutrients it needs to function at its peak.

It's tempting to assume that school-aged children just don't drink to the sort of degree that would impair their learning. But don't be complacent. I know of one head teacher who took charge of a secondary school in Birmingham, and found that his first task was to stamp out a culture of alcohol abuse. Around a quarter of the pupils were drinking regularly, many of them *during* the school day. Some were drinking during lunch break, some were skipping lessons in the afternoon. And plenty more were drinking out of school and turning up for lessons hung over and bleary-eyed.

It's an extreme example. Most teenagers don't drink in school, and they rarely drink on a night before school. Many drink sensibly, and in moderation. But the reality is that you should probably be more concerned about your child drinking alcohol than about them taking drugs. The statistics make grim reading. Around 11 per cent of thirteen-year-olds and 28 per cent of fifteen-year-olds admit to getting drunk once a week. In the last fifteen years underage consumption of alcohol has doubled. A quarter of Year 11 pupils admit to three or more binge-drinking sessions each month. It's easier, and cheaper, than ever for children to get hold of alcohol. And many see it as a 'soft' crime, something that doesn't really matter that will have little or no long-term effect.

So what are the risks? The problem is that no one really knows. Most research into the effects of alcohol on the body and brain has focused on adults rather than children. But many scientists believe that alcohol is generally more harmful to young people because their bodies and brains are still developing. When it comes to children of thirteen or fourteen years old it's hard to be sure exactly what moderation means.

Then there are the knock-on effects that heavy drinking can have. A third of twelve- to seventeen-year-olds admit committing acts of vandalism or getting into arguments or fights after drinking alcohol. And the UK's high rates of teenage pregnancy are almost certainly linked to the high rates of teenage drunkenness, with one in seven teenagers saying they have had unprotected sex while being drunk.

Apologies for bombarding you with statistics, but they do seem to tell their own story. If your child is going to fulfil her potential at school, then regular heavy drinking isn't a good idea.

The best advice is to try to educate your child about the risks of alcohol, and to encourage sensible drinking habits. Telling a sixteen-year-old not to drink probably won't work. But encouraging her to stick within sensible limits is important. You need to set a good example. Introducing young people to alcohol in a safe, controlled setting – such as family meals – makes good sense. It's also helpful if you can persuade teenagers to stick to drinks with lower levels of alcohol, and discourage them from drinking on an empty stomach.

> **Did You Know?**
>
> The most common alcoholic drinks among thirteen- to fifteen-year-olds are fruit-flavoured 'alcopops'. These typically have an alcoholic strength of between 5 and 6 per cent, meaning they contain more alcohol than a half pint of beer or a single shot of spirits.

SELF-HARM

Cutting, stabbing, burning, bruising. Finding out that your child deliberately harms her own body can be shocking and distressing. The parental instinct is to protect your child. Yet here you are, unable even to protect her from herself.

It's easy to think that this will never happen. It's not like binge drinking or bullying, which is in the papers and on the news. It may not be something you've seen for yourself. You may think it's not an issue for schools. But it's not such an unlikely scenario as you might imagine. Self-harm is on the increase. It's estimated that around one in ten children self-harms at some point during their teenage years, but the figure is higher among girls, and in certain parts of the country. Research in Edinburgh, for example, found that nearly a third of fifteen-year-old girls had inflicted physical pain on themselves, usually through cutting their arms or legs with a knife.

Most children who self-harm never tell their parents. Self-harm is rarely a cry for help. It is not meant to be discovered. It usually takes place in private, or in the company of other self-harmers, and young people often go to great lengths to keep it secret. You're more likely to find out by chance, or by noticing marks on your child's body. I know one mum who only realised there was a problem when her daughter wore long-sleeved tops right through a heat wave.

If you do find out that your child is cutting herself, don't be disgusted. Or angry. There are many different reasons why children self-harm. The only way to find out why your child does it is to talk to her, and this is best done as calmly as possible. In most cases self-harm is a way of coping with distress. It could be linked to worry about exams, relationships, weight or physical appearance; in fact, any of the usual teenage concerns. It's not meant to shock you, and even though it probably will, you should try to deal with it as you would any other serious emotional crisis.

But why choose to deal with emotional pain by causing physical pain? Many self-harmers say it makes them feel in control of one small part of their lives. Cutting themselves is performed as a ritual, with careful preparation and cleaning up afterwards. Others say it brings feelings of relief and takes their mind off other things. And others just say it makes them feel good. When we are in pain our bodies release endorphins, a kind of natural painkiller. Controlled pain can actually produce a feel-good factor, which explains why some people find it as addictive as drinking or smoking.

The first reaction to discovering that your child self-harms could well be shame. You could feel that you've let your child down, or failed somehow as a parent. But while it's natural to feel this way, it's not useful, especially if it stops you seeking outside help. Putting your child in touch with a professional may be the best way forward. You have to place your child's needs ahead of any embarrassment you might be feeling. And you'll soon find that you're not alone. There are support groups dedicated to helping children who self-harm and their families. Being able to talk to other people who share the same feelings may be enough to stop your child hurting herself, and may help you cope with your reactions.

There's no 'cure' for self-harm, but it's often possible to find a more healthy way of responding to emotional pain. It will take time, and you can't hope to change the way your child thinks overnight. But work on building self-esteem, and make sure you offer all the support you can. Most experts say the worst thing you can do is to order your child to stop, or confiscate the equipment she uses. In the short term self-harm is a way of coping with problems. If you take that away before the problems have been addressed, then you take away her way of coping. Remember, self-harm isn't about self-destruction, it's about self-protection. So however hard it seems, try to look at the positives.

Did You Know?

- The UK has the highest rate of self-harm in Europe.
- Around 24,000 under-eighteens are treated in casualty departments every year as the result of self-inflicted injuries.
- Girls are four times more likely than boys to self-harm.
- Self-harm isn't just something that teenagers do. There are people in their sixties and seventies who still inflict injury on themselves. And children as young as five sometimes self-harm, by deliberately grazing their knees or banging their heads against a wall.

TAKING DRUGS

'Everyone else's child takes drugs.'

'My child never would.'

If those two statements sum up your view of teenagers and illegal drugs then you need to think again.

Regular drug use among young people isn't as common as you might believe. In a recent survey by ICM only 13 per cent of eleven- to sixteen-year-olds said they had taken drugs. And in 85 per cent of cases the only drug they had taken was cannabis. The findings of the survey weren't unusual. Research consistently shows that a majority of children don't take drugs. Of those that do, most are occasional users of cannabis. The number of children who use 'hard' drugs or who could be deemed to have a 'drug problem' is very small indeed.

Now the bad news. You might assume your child hasn't taken drugs, but that doesn't mean you're right. The same ICM survey reveals that, more often than not, parents are unaware that their children have taken drugs. You may think you know what your son or daughter gets up to. The truth is, you don't.

This book isn't about parenting in its widest sense. It's about helping your child succeed at school. What young people do in their spare time may have very little impact on how they fare in the classroom. If your teenage son smokes cannabis on a Saturday night every now and then, it's unlikely to send his grades tumbling into freefall. But a holistic approach to children's wellbeing means looking at every angle. And there's growing evidence that regular cannabis use can have an adverse effect on short-term memory and concentration span. Susan Greenfield, Oxford professor in synaptic pharmacology, believes cannabis use may cause changes in the pattern of networks that connect brain cells, so lowering levels of motivation. And stronger strains of cannabis – usually known as skunk – have been linked to an increased risk of psychosis and schizophrenia. Then, of course, there's the fact that every year several hundred young people are excluded from school, because they're caught in possession of drugs or under the influence. And being thrown out clearly isn't very 'School Smart'!

If you want to minimise the chances of your child taking drugs then it makes sense to talk to them about drug use in an honest and open way. Trying to frighten someone away from drugs isn't a good idea. Drug-taking has its risks, but you should never exaggerate the dangers. Otherwise, when your child sees her friends taking drugs without obvious ill effects, it undermines what you've said. You lose credibility. And she will be less likely to trust your advice in the future. Information has to be accurate and up to date. If you want to talk to your child about drug use, then do your research thoroughly.

Many parents worry that peer pressure will force their child to try drugs. It's true that some young people do get talked into things by their friends, often against their judgement. All you can do is make sure that your child knows the statistics about drug use. If she knows that most children don't take drugs, then she's less likely to feel under pressure. You can even practise role-play where your child can explore ways of turning down drugs without losing face with her friends. Some schools have now introduced random drug-testing, not because they're determined to catch drug-users, but because the tests give other children an excuse to say no.

If you *do* find out that your child has taken drugs, then the initial advice is much the same as for dealing with bullying or self-harm, or any other serious family issue. It's important to stay calm and to talk openly. You need to establish what drugs have been used, and whether your child is a first-time user, an occasional user or a regular user. Only then can you gauge an appropriate response. If there are any indications that your child's wellbeing is adversely affected by drugs then you're absolutely right to be concerned. If it's just a case of them experimenting once or twice then you'll need to handle things sensitively. Drugs can be devastating. And if you want your child to perform to the best of her academic ability then anything that affects the brain has to be taken seriously. But I would hazard a guess that more teenagers do badly at school because of underlying friction between themselves and their parents, than do badly at school because of occasional recreational drug use. So tread carefully.

Did You Know?

- Over a quarter of parents feel they don't know enough about drugs to talk about them with their child – and would rather someone else did it.
- 20 per cent of parents admit they would 'lose their rag' if they discovered their child had been taking drugs.

- Children are actually good at 'saying no'. A survey in Scotland found that 34 per cent of thirteen-year-olds said they had been offered a drug, but only 13 per cent said they had used a drug.
- The idea that cannabis use leads to harder drugs is unfounded, according to most recent research.

12. MAKING THE MOST OF TALENT: THE X-FACTORS THAT MATTER

Matthew's jogging along nicely at school. He does what he's told, and he does the work his teachers set him. But his parents are concerned that he doesn't really seem engaged with what he's doing. He's just going through the motions. There's not much commitment or motivation. There's not much enthusiasm. He's easily distracted and he doesn't seem to be responding any more to their encouragement.

We all have days when we'd rather be shopping or sunbathing than working. But how do you keep your child interested day in, day out, during the long school terms? Having a talented child is one thing. But to get the most from his talent he'll need to learn to concentrate and focus; to motivate himself; and to feel comfortable with who he is and what he's doing.

CONCENTRATION

Concentration is one of the cornerstones of learning. It allows children to work in an efficient, directed way. It keeps their attention focused in class. And if you can build up your child's concentration levels, you're likely to see big improvements in the way he learns and studies.

Some grown-ups are convinced that children's attention spans are getting shorter all the time. It's usually modern technology that gets the blame. It's true that when young people watch TV or surf the net, they flick from channel to channel, or click from page to page. But that's not necessarily because their attention span is short. It's because most children are now able to make on-the-spot critical decisions. 'Is this something I'm interested in? Is this something I want to watch?' If the answer is 'no' they move on. That's not a problem with their attention span; it's actually a very useful life skill. On the other hand, adults often sit staring at TV programmes they have no real interest in. Does it mean they have amazing powers of concentration? No. It means they're just too tired to change channels.

When young people do find something they're interested in, they are often able to concentrate for long periods of time. They may play a new video game for hours on end as they attempt to master it. They don't have any problem watching a two-hour film, as long as it's good enough. They have high demands, but as long as those demands are met, they're happy to pay some attention. Children are used to all-action video games and special effects. They're used to being able to skip through the boring bits. So perhaps it's understandable if a teacher standing and talking at the front of a class doesn't hold their attention. But that's not the child's fault – it's the teacher's. It means they have to work a bit harder – and sharpen up their act.

What's important is that children are able to concentrate when they *need* to, not just when they *want* to. The teacher droning on at the front of the class may seem dull, but what they're saying could be important. So how can children learn to hold their concentration? How can they stay focused on that maths homework when their friends or siblings are outside playing football or upstairs playing loud music?

Keeping concentration levels high is often a matter of willpower. It's a skill that can be learned. The first thing to understand is that losing concentration is perfectly normal. From time to time we all find that we've been staring blankly at the page while dreaming of a sunny beach. Or that someone's been speaking to us, but we're not quite sure what they've said. The trick is to realise when your attention has drifted and to get your focus back as quickly as possible.

Taking regular breaks is important. If your child feels his concentration levels slipping then he should take a rest and come back refreshed. But it can also be useful to try to extend the natural attention span. A teenager revising for an exam might find that working in fifteen-minute blocks is best. And that's fine. But stretching the study periods to twenty minutes, or maybe twenty-five minutes, should be an achievable goal. It takes willpower though, and practice. A common strategy is to repeat a mantra to yourself when you feel your attention slipping: 'Five More Minutes!' 'Stay Focused!'

The problem is that this kind of routine can lead to clock-watching. And that can provide an excuse for having a breather when you'd be better off pushing on for a few more minutes. Taking a break because you really need a break is fine, but taking a break because the clock says you should – and because what you're doing is boring you to tears – is just another way of time-wasting. Concentration dips can be a form of mental laziness. Sometimes you need to rest; sometimes you need to buckle down. Deep concentration comes when you get caught up in what you're doing, and stopping and starting every ten minutes won't help. It's best if your child works until he feels like a break, rather than deciding in advance to take a break every twenty minutes. Our attention spans vary depending on our mood and on what we're doing. So working in a fixed way doesn't make much sense.

Often what seems like a problem with concentration can actually be a problem with the task in hand. If your child seems unable to concentrate on a piece of work, then it may be because he feels daunted by it. Or bored by it.

If that's the case then breaking up the work into smaller, more manageable chunks may help. Or he could try starting with the bits he finds easiest or most interesting, to help get focused. Sometimes children need to change their mind-set. Instead of thinking, 'I need to finish this piece of work,' they could try thinking, 'I need to work on this for half an hour and then see how far I've got.' Putting in the time becomes the focus of their efforts – and that's always an achievable goal. Children usually find that this kind of approach takes the pressure off. They're often surprised how far they get in the time, and how less daunting it seems at the end of it.

Being properly motivated certainly helps us to concentrate. I taught one boy who had difficulty staying focused in class. His parents were convinced that he simply wasn't capable of concentrating. 'He's just the same at home,' they said. But one Saturday afternoon, I watched the lad play cricket and score a half-century. He batted for over two hours without making any mistakes. He could concentrate well enough when the desire and motivation was there.

Many children find it easier to focus when there are no distractions. But it's important that they learn to concentrate even with other people around them. Being able to shut out distractions is invaluable in a noisy classroom. It's also pretty handy later in life. The first time I spent a day working in an open-plan office, I struggled to get anything done. I was constantly looking at what was going on around me and it took a while to adjust. But, with practice, most people can acquire some kind of tunnel vision. The important thing is not to be wound up by factors you can't control. If other people are being noisy you probably can't stop them. But you can learn to ignore them. Footballers often play in front of thousands of people, who might be shouting and hurling abuse. The best players just stay focused on what they're doing.

Studying can be hard work. School can sometimes be boring. Everybody's concentration slips eventually. The important thing is to encourage your child to think about how they like to work, and how they work best. Once they become aware of how they learn, the chances are they'll become better learners.

Things To Do

There are lots of games and exercises that can help improve concentration. As with other exercises in the book, not everyone will find all of the exercises helpful. It's a question of giving them a try, and seeing what works for you and your child.

- Get your child to sit comfortably or lie on the floor. Ask them to listen carefully to the sounds they can hear. Then ask them to focus only on the sounds that are *inside* the room, shutting out the sounds from outside. After a minute, ask them to focus instead only on noises from *outside* the room.
- Encourage your child to spend time looking very closely at an object for several minutes. For starters, get him to hold his hand out in front of his face and look at it closely for one minute. He'll become aware of the details of the hand – the lines and patterns on the skin. When he finds his attention wandering in other situations, he may be able to look at his hand for just a few seconds and feel refocused.
- Mime is an excellent way of improving concentration, and great fun. Even just miming a simple task such as putting on a shirt takes a great deal of concentration if it's to be convincing.

- Encourage your child to focus on his breathing. Get him to breathe slowly in and out. In through the nose for a count of four. Then out through the mouth, also for a count of four. Start off by counting aloud, to help your child. After a minute, stop counting. Your child should stay focused on his breathing and stay relaxed.
- Ask your child to try and draw three perfect circles by hand (or as near to perfect as possible!). They should all be exactly the same size. You'll find that drawing slowly needs a good deal of concentration.

These exercises work well with younger children. Older children may prefer activities or sports that boost concentration. Chess is a good example. So too are t'ai chi, yoga or martial arts, and sports such as fencing, shooting or archery.

STAYING FOCUSED: IDEAS FOR A BREAK

In the middle of a homework assignment that's due within hours, or when your child is losing interest in painting every stripe in the world's major flags, it's not very convenient to break off for a bracing walk or a quick run around the playing fields. Yet sometimes that's exactly the kind of thing that's needed: a physical boost to relax the brain, refocus and get moving again. We all know that a long day in a stuffy classroom or a lengthy study session at home can leave us feeling foggy and our concentration levels low, but it's not always easy to shake off the effects.

One solution to this conundrum was developed in the US in the 1970s by Dr Paul Dennison. He knew already that physical exercise is good for the brain. And that mental exercise is good for the brain. So why not put the two together? That's the thinking behind Brain Gym. His exercises were later trademarked and now they're used in thousands of schools across the world. In recent years, other people have also developed their own body-brain exercises along similar lines.

Brain Gym combines physical and mental activity. Unlike just jumping up and down on the spot, the exercises are focused and require a degree of concentration. Some of the routines involve massaging points of the body to improve blood flow. Others are simple co-ordination exercises, like rubbing your stomach with one hand while patting your head with the other. Or writing your name in the air, first using one hand, then the other, then both together.

These body-brain exercises are designed to wake up the mind, so that when children start to learn they'll be more alert and receptive. In the long term, it's claimed that regular Brain Gym can build up the neural pathways, improving memory, concentration, and reading and writing skills, not to mention self-esteem and athleticism.

That all sounds very impressive. But does it actually work? Once again, there's a big gap between what people who use body-brain exercises believe, and what the scientists have to say.

The theory behind body-brain routines seems reasonable enough. The basic idea is that brain function is intimately connected to movement. Every move we make begins life as an impulse in the brain. And movement is important to the learning process. As babies we discover the world not through words, but by exploring it and touching it. By moving. So even as we get older we should perhaps use movement to stimulate the brain and develop our abilities.

Teachers who use Brain Gym in schools seem to like it. No surprise there. If they didn't like it, they wouldn't use it. But children also seem to enjoy it, and many people are convinced it makes a difference. The Department of Education and Skills even promotes a Brain Gym book on its website. It has become very popular in primary schools, and some secondary schools use it too, especially in the run-up to exams. Some schools have Brain Gym at the start of the day – others use it in the middle of lessons, when concentration starts to sag, and the class begins to lose focus. Teachers claim that it changes the atmosphere in the room, and gives everyone more energy. And yes, over time, they say that children's work also improves.

But many people argue that the whole thing is a sham, with no scientific basis. There's very little evidence that certain physical movements boost our capacity to solve maths problems, for example. Or that we can improve blood flow to very specific areas of the brain, or that we can become more clever by somehow encouraging the left and right sides of our brain to work together. We just don't understand the brain well enough to be able to back up these claims. Most of the research to date has relied on asking teachers and children how they feel and whether they *think* the exercises are doing them good. And while many people swear by body-brain exercises, they'd probably find that even just standing up and walking around for a bit would have the same effect. Any kind of physical activity is likely to sharpen up our concentration. Taking a break is bound to help us relax, especially if we do a bit of stretching and listen to some soothing music.

There's no reason why you can't encourage your child to do body-brain exercises at home. Most of the routines are simple enough. And while there's no scientific proof that these exercises work, that doesn't mean we can say for sure that they don't. They're good fun and can't do any harm. But don't tell your child that body-brain exercises will make him smarter, because there's no real evidence. Instead, just say, 'This is something you might find helpful.' Let him make up his own mind about whether the exercises are a gimmick or a good thing.

If you want to try a session down the Brain Gym, then fine. But it might prove just as helpful to encourage your child to put together his own routine of exercises that he can turn to when his concentration needs a lift, especially something that can be done outside in the fresh air. Try for more than aimlessly kicking a ball around. Look at borrowing some moves from t'ai chi or yoga, or relaxation routines. Try to create something structured. Add music if it helps. And be practical: you want something fairly quick and easy that your child can do on his own when he needs to and that will refocus his attention, not distract him for ages.

Things To Do

Here are some simple body-brain activities you can teach your child:

- Rub your stomach with one hand and pat your head with the other. Then swap them over.
- March around the room. Swing your left arm forward as your left leg goes forward, and your right arm forward with your right leg. After thirty seconds or so, change so that your arms swing forward with the opposite leg.
- Place your left hand out in front of you, level with your eyes. Move it very slowly and smoothly to the left, and watch it closely as it goes, turning your head. When that becomes uncomfortable, put your left hand behind your back and put your right hand in front of your eyes. Move it slowly and smoothly to the right, watching it carefully. Continue changing hands for two to three minutes.
- Draw a letter from the alphabet in the air with your left index finger. Then draw the next letter of the alphabet on the floor with your right foot. Then the next letter with your right index finger in the air. Then the next with your left foot on the floor. Finally, walk round the room tracing the outline of the next letter with your steps.

Next Steps

If you want to find out more about the official Brain Gym™ programme then go to www.braingym.org.uk.

There are lots of activities that can stimulate the mind and improve co-ordination. Tap-dancing is a great one. So is learning to play a musical instrument. And t'ai chi combines fluid movements and controlled breathing. These activities might prove to be more fun for your child than just doing body-brain exercises and may have similar benefits in terms of promoting relaxation and concentration.

PROMPTS AND CHALLENGES

Children ask a lot of questions. It's their way of making sense of the world. Sometimes they ask so many that it drives you up the wall. But try not to discourage them, even if it can be wearing at times. The questions your child asks will give you a valuable insight into how his mind works. And remember, the world would probably be a better place if adults showed the same curiosity and thirst for knowledge.

Of course, some of the questions children ask are tricky. Why is grass green? What are clouds made of? Why does cheese smell? You won't always have the answer. In which case, don't be afraid to admit it. Perhaps it's the perfect opportunity for some family research. 'I don't know, but let's find out!' is more fun than 'Oh, who cares?' By being curious yourself, you show your child that learning is desirable and fun.

Things To Do

Play games that show children questions can be fun. One favourite is Twenty Questions: the first player has to think of a person, place or thing. The second player has to find out what it is. They ask the first player a question, to which the answer must be yes or no. They have up to twenty questions to try to find out what the other player has in mind. As children get better at the game they will ask more useful questions, which help them narrow down the options.

Encouraging your child to ask questions at home will give them the confidence to ask questions at school. And that's important. At the age of five children ask as many as fifty questions a day. They are curious about the world. They want answers. But studies show that once children go to primary school, the number of questions they ask drops sharply. Why is that? Could it be that children suddenly become less inquisitive and lose their curiosity? Or that the world suddenly makes sense, and they no longer need to ask about things? Unlikely.

People love questions. That's why there are so many quiz shows on television. Even if we don't know many of the answers, we're happy to watch. The one place people don't like questions is at school. Hardly surprising. There are tests and exams, for a start, which are generally seen as scary and unpleasant. Then there's the potential embarrassment of being asked a question in front of your classmates and not knowing the answer. Or worse still, deciding to *ask* a question that the rest of the class finds obvious or stupid. And teachers often make matters worse. Some of them use questions aggressively, as a way of keeping control. Not paying attention at the back? Then expect a tricky question to come shooting your way. Other teachers just don't understand the value of questions. They drone on for most of the lesson, and then just as the bell rings and everyone's ready to head off for break, they call out, 'Any questions?' And what they really mean, of course, is: 'There aren't any questions, are there?' Questions are made to look like an irrelevance or an interruption, nothing more than an afterthought.

So all too often questions turn into something that children are afraid of asking, and afraid of being asked. When they should really be something to be enjoyed.

> ### Things To Do
>
> Instead of asking your child whether they learned anything at school, ask them whether they asked any good questions. It will help get across the idea that questions are just as important as answers.

The best teachers turn their classrooms into a 'community of enquiry'. That is to say, a place where everybody feels comfortable and confident about asking questions. A place where children are encouraged to think for themselves, rather than being spoon-fed. And where teacher and pupils work together towards the answers. With the right attitude, there's no reason why you can't turn your home into a similar community of enquiry. And if you want to encourage your child to think more deeply about the world around them, then what you really need to do is prompt and challenge them, not give them all the answers.

It's helpful to think of questions as falling into two different categories. Lower-order questions are ones that require children to recall information. They are usually 'closed' questions, with a right or wrong answer. Something like 'What's the capital of Spain?' or 'Is that the last chocolate bar you're eating?' Higher-order questions are more complex and actually require children to do some thinking. They tend to be 'open questions' that can't just be answered with a simple yes or no. In the course of an average day, most people ask, and get asked, an awful lot of lower-order questions. But it's the higher-order questions that really develop children's mental powers. As a simple rule, asking your child questions that begin with 'how', 'which' or 'why' is a sure-fire way to get them thinking.

Things To Do

- Try asking higher-order questions that start with 'how' or 'why'.
- Try to engage older children in debate. That means getting them to question their own views, and those of other people. Useful questions to have up your sleeve might be:
  - Why do you think that?
  - How do you know that?
  - What do you mean by that?
- Remember that children sometimes just need simple, straightforward answers. Always being evasive, or answering questions with another question, may make your child less curious. Be challenging, but don't be unhelpful!

Whatever kind of questions you ask your child, it's important to give them time to think about the answer. Some questions have preoccupied philosophers for a lifetime or spanned centuries of civilisation. Life after death? The chicken or the egg? The sound of one hand clapping? Yet in day-to-day life, most people who ask a question expect an answer in less than a second. It's hardly likely to encourage deep thinking.

Try not to fall into the trap of answering your own questions, just because you don't get an instant reply. If you give your child the answer every time he looks at you blankly, you won't be stretching his mind. Waiting just three seconds will give your child time to think. Waiting five seconds will give him time to think and then reflect on his initial thoughts. But sometimes it's good to leave children pondering a question for much longer. Overnight, perhaps, or for a few days. Over that time you can revisit the idea, with different prompts, to help him explore new angles.

Let's suppose you ask your child why different countries are in different time zones. After all, you suggest, wouldn't it be easier if it was the same time all over the world? That might take some puzzling over. For you, as well as your child! And you could offer prompts such as, 'What would happen in Australia if school hours fell during the night?' or 'What do we need daylight for anyway?' Taking time to think things through is important if children are fully to develop their thought processes. It proves to them that the best answers are not always the quickest ones; and that the best questions deserve respect and reflection.

Next Steps

Professor Robert Fisher, of the University of Brunel, has published a whole range of books designed to get children thinking. Some are stories or poems, others contain ideas for games. They're aimed at seven- to fourteen-year-olds and are a good way of developing thinking and discussion. See www.teachingthinking.net for more details.

MOTIVATION

You know that your child will learn best when he's motivated. He'll pay better attention if he's enthusiastic. He'll work for longer if he's keen. But where does motivation come from? Why can some children summon up enthusiasm for the dullest of lessons while others only spark into life once or twice a week?

Motivation can take many forms. Psychologists have identified two basic types, what they call 'intrinsic motivation' and 'extrinsic motivation'. When you offer your child a reward, or threaten them with a punishment, then that's extrinsic motivation. It's the old-fashioned idea of carrot and stick. The other kind of motivation is intrinsic motivation,

motivation that comes from within. Perhaps the desire to do the work for its own sake, or because you feel pride in your work; or because you recognise the benefits of working well and winning success.

Of course, that's the motivation you're after. Intrinsic motivation is the Holy Grail. But it sounds too idealistic, doesn't it? Well, sometimes it is. Not all the schoolwork children do is going to excite them. Many parents encourage their children to work by promising them rewards – motivation by money. I've known parents offer their kids £10 for every good grade on a piece of homework. And when it comes to exam time, the prizes on offer get bigger and better. A games console? A new bike? A trip to Disneyland? A car? It sounds more like a quiz show than an education. And schools are as much to blame as parents. Good work is rewarded with stars, house points or treats. Some even pay out cash to children who do well in exams. The problem with offering constant rewards is that it turns education into a results business. In any game show there are losers. Children who don't do so well feel like failures.

At the other end of the scale, if children are motivated by rewards rather than by the ideal of doing their best, then they're likely to do only as much as they need to. Why should a child really stretch himself if he can get an A grade by learning the right answers by rote and churning them out in the exam hall? And if young people get used to short-term rewards, how will they develop the motivation and persistence to work towards long-term goals? How will they react when there are no rewards on offer? Too many rewards and the message is clear: it's results that matter, not the process of learning and developing your mind. And that's a dangerous message to send out.

External motivating factors are important. They reinforce the idea that it feels good to succeed, even if it's only because there's more money in your pocket. But they should be used occasionally and wisely: the ultimate goal is to get your child motivating himself, and enjoying his work for what it is. Most young children are naturally intrinsically motivated. They find the world challenging and interesting. But a few years with the pressures of school can easily dampen all this enthusiasm. If you feel your child is starting to lose interest in learning for its own sake then here are a few things to try.

Firstly, have a look at your own attitudes. Are you setting a good example? Are you, at least sometimes, still curious and enthusiastic about the world? Secondly, try and sound out your child as to why he finds it hard to get excited about his schoolwork. There may be a variety of reasons, but lack of intrinsic motivation often arises from a couple of basic things: not getting appropriate challenges from the work (that is, it's either too hard or too easy), or not feeling in control of the work.

Once you've got a better idea about what might be behind your child's lack of enthusiasm, then you can try to find a solution. One way is to make the work more personal and relevant. There's bound to be something that gets your child intrinsically motivated, even if it's not homework. By drawing on this enthusiasm you can help your child see that he can make a positive choice, within the boundaries of the task. So perhaps your child has to write a story. And he hates writing stories. But he loves bird-watching. By writing a story about bird-watching, he feels he's got an element of control over what he's doing. There may still be spelling and grammar to struggle with, but if you set a realistic goal – to explain the best way to watch birds – then he can feel pride in doing that part of the work well.

Another strategy worth trying is to emphasise the long-term benefits of getting the work done. Shift the emphasis from this piece of work, which may be too boring for words, to the idea of what ultimate success might mean. A good piece of work, leading to good grades, leading to good exam results, leading to a good job, with good money, etc., etc. It may seem obvious, but children who have learned to recognise the benefits of success, and relate them to what they are doing, are much more likely to be intrinsically motivated.

And if all else fails? There's always the lure of a trip to the cinema or a crisp tenner!

SELF-ESTEEM

No one wants their child to be arrogant or conceited. But it's important that children feel loved and aware of their worth. Children with high self-esteem find it easier to cope with the knock-backs at school. They find it easier to make friends, and are more likely to be motivated to do well. When the going gets tough they persevere, where other children might just give up.

You don't have to constantly tell your child that he's wonderful. You can build his self-esteem simply by spending time with him, and showing him respect. By listening to him carefully, giving him eye contact, and making it clear that you love him. By helping him build a good group of friends. By giving him freedom and responsibility to make his own decisions. By showing that you trust him.

Don't let children fall into the trap of becoming constantly self-critical, or feeling down about themselves. Every child has strengths and weaknesses. Human nature means we often get hung up about our failings, so you may sometimes need to help your child focus on what he's good at. If you yourself have a positive can-do attitude, then that will rub off on your child.

Finally, when you have to be critical of your child then always tread carefully. Never criticise him as a person, only criticise his actions. Don't say, 'You're selfish.' Instead say, 'What you did just then was selfish.' And try to end with something positive, offering ideas for how he could have handled the situation differently.

PRAISE

Human beings are incredibly sensitive to both praise and criticism. It's rare for anyone – let alone a child – to be immune. Being praised makes us feel good. Being criticised makes us feel bad. Most parents know that it's important to praise their children, and that it's best to go easy on the negative comments. But too much praise can actually be just as stunting and damaging as too much criticism.

The danger with constant praise is that it can make children afraid to fail. They become praise-junkies who are addicted to success. They may even start to avoid doing things they are no good at, just because they don't like to fail. They choose to do the things they think they are good at, rather than the things they really enjoy. Yet taking risks and failing is important. It's a valuable part of the learning process. It's the only way to really stretch and challenge ourselves; to find out more about our abilities. Oddly, the child who is constantly praised and told that he's clever can end up lacking in confidence. It's quite logical, if you think about it. If your child does well and you tell him it's because he's clever, then when he does badly he will think it's because he's stupid.

In the US, a team of researchers at Columbia University carried out an experiment to judge the effects of different kinds of praise. A group of children took a test. When they got their results they were either praised for being clever, or praised for their effort. They were then offered the chance to do another test and they could choose between a test of the same standard or a harder test. Children who had been praised for their effort tended to choose the harder test. But among the children who had been praised for being clever, a majority opted for the same level of difficulty. They simply wanted to repeat their success and get praised again – they didn't want to stretch themselves. What's more, when all the children went back to doing an easy test, those who had been praised for their effort did better than the first time, while those who had been praised for their intelligence did worse. Either they were putting in less effort, because they thought they had it sorted, or they felt under too much pressure to do as well as the previous time. Either way, the experiment suggested that telling children they were clever didn't really help them.

There's no doubt that praise can help motivate children. But it has to be sincere. Children can tell when adults are just trying to cheer them up or jolly them along. It makes praise meaningless. Worse still, if you always use praise as a pick-me-up or confidence booster, then children may even learn to associate it with failure. But praising your child can be addictive. For some parents, praising their child actually becomes a form of praising themselves. 'You're a great child' isn't that far removed from 'I'm a great parent'.

But that's not to say that praise isn't important. Used well it encourages children and raises their self-esteem. Praise your child for their effort, not just for what they achieve. Make sure that praise is specific, so it becomes a useful form of feedback. 'I like the colour you used in that painting.' 'There's not one spelling mistake in that story.' 'That's a very original idea.'

And try to mix praise with constructive criticism sometimes, because that sends out the message that you believe your child can do better – that you have high expectations. If you only praise and never criticise, your child may think you have low expectations of them.

It's a minefield, isn't it? All you can do – as with most of the topics covered in this book – is try to be sincere and, above all, positive.

FURTHER READING

Brain and Intelligence

The 21st Century Brain, Steven Rose (Vintage Books, 2005)
A User's Guide to the Brain, John Ratey (Abacus, 2001)
Intelligence Reframed, Howard Gardner (Basic Books, 1999)
The New Brain: How the Modern Age is Rewiring Your Mind,
  Richard Restak (Rodale, 2004)
The Private Life of the Brain, Susan Greenfield (Penguin,
  2002)
Emotional Intelligence, Daniel Goleman (Bantam, 1997)

Schools

The Good Schools Guide, Ralph Lucas (Lucas, 2007)
The Independent Schools Guide, Gabbitas (Kogan Page, 2006)
A Parent's Guide to Primary School, Katy Byrne and Harvey
  McGavin (Continuum, 2004)

Parenting

The Confident Child, Terri Apter (WW Norton, 2007)
The Hurried Child: Growing Up Too Fast Too Soon, David
  Elkind (Da Capo, 2001)
*Hothouse Kids: How the Pressure to Succeed Is Threatening
  Childhood,* Alissa Quart, (Arrow, 2007)
Flying Start: Coaching Your Children for Life, Emma Sargent
  (Cyan, 2006)
How to Raise a Bright Child, Joan Freeman (Vermilion, 1996)

Study Skills

The Buzan Study Skills Handbook, Tony Buzan (BBC Active,
  2006)
Use Your Head, Tony Buzan (BBC Active, 2003)

Mind Maps for Kids, Tony Buzan (Harper Collins, 2003)
Use Your Memory, Tony Buzan (BBC Active, 1993)
Thinking Skills and Eye Q, Oliver Caviglioli, Ian Harris and Bill Tindall (Network Educational Press, 2002)
Handwriting: The Way to Teach It, Rosemary Sassoon (Paul Chapman, 2003)
The Homework Myth, Alfie Kohn (Da Capo Press, 2007)
Building Learning Power, Guy Claxton (TLO, 2002)
Stories for Thinking, Robert Fisher (Nash Pollock, 1996)
Teaching Children to Think, Robert Fisher (Nelson Thornes, 2005)

Wellbeing

Toxic Childhood: How the Modern World Is Damaging Our Children and What We Can Do about It, Sue Palmer, Orion (2006)
Understanding Street Drugs: A Handbook of Substance Misuse for Parents, Teachers and Other Professionals, David Emmett and Graeme Nice (Jessica Kingsley, 2005)
They Are What You Feed Them, Alex Richardson (Harper Collins, 2006)
The Dinner Lady: Change the Way Your Children Eat, for Life, Jeanette Orrey (Bantam, 2005)

RESEARCH

Throughout *School Smart*, where I've referred to research or quoted facts and figures, I've tended not to specify names, dates and places. I wanted the book to be accessible, comfortable reading – and unfortunately academic papers often have rather wordy titles. But here's a list of studies and surveys that have been cited.

Chapter Basics

Fertile Minds, JM Nash, Baylor College of Medicine, Texas (1997)

Piano Training and Math Puzzle Solving, G Shaw, University Of California, Irvine (1999)

Music and Spatial Task Performance, G Shaw and K Ky, University Of California, Irvine (1993)

Survey of head teachers by National Literacy Trust (2003)

Survey of primary teachers' handwriting training by Institute of Education, London, 2006

Research into 'maths anxiety', S Ford, University of Staffordshire (2005)

The Effects of Synthetic Phonics Teaching on Reading and Spelling Attainment, R Johnston and J Watson, St Andrew's University (2005)

The Brain

Attaining Excellence Through Deliberate Practice, KA Ericcson, Florida State University (2002)

Understanding the Brain: Towards a New Learning Science, OECD, 2002

The Neurological Basis of Intelligence: A Contrast with 'Brain-based' Education, JG Geake, Oxford Brookes University, 2005

Motivation

Praise for Intelligence Can Undermine Children's Motivation and Performance, CM Mueller, Columbia University, 1997

Nutrition, Rest and Exercise

Breakfast Reduces Decline in Attention and Memory over the Morning in Schoolchildren, KA Wesnes et al. (2003)

National Diet and Nutrition Survey (2000)

Health Trends Survey, Department of Health (2005)

Various studies, A Kelley, Wisconsin University (2002)

A Drink of Water Can Improve or Impair Mental Performance Depending on Small Differences in Thirst, PJ Rogers et al. (2001)

Hydration and Cognitive Function in Children, KE D'Anci et al. (2006)

Omega-3 Fatty Acids in ADHD and Related Neuro-developmental Disorders, AJ Richardson (2006)

The Oxford–Durham Study: a randomized controlled trial of dietary supplementation with fatty acids in children with developmental coordination disorder, AJ Richardson and P Montgomery (2005)

Research into the link between sleep and memory, M Walker et al. (Harvard, 2003)

Research into link between exercise and brain-cell growth, Scott Small, (Columbia University, 2007)

Emotional Intelligence

Various studies, Roy Baumeister, Case Western Reserve University (2002)

The Right School

Attitudes Towards Independent Schools, MORI (2003)

Various studies of the effects of setting in schools, S Hallam and J Ireson, Institute of Education, London (2001)

Private Tuition and Home Education

Research into benefits of private tuition, J Ireson, Institute of Education, London (2005)

Home Schooling: From the Extreme to the Mainstream, The Fraser Institute (2001)

Home Schooling Achievement, National Home Education Research Institute (2001)

Home-Education: comparison of home and school educated children on PIPS Baseline Assessments, P Rothermel, (University of Durham, 2004)

Study Skills

The Efficacy of the 'Mind Map' Study Technique, P Farrand, F Hussain and E Hennessy (2002)

What Can Go Wrong

Bullying: How to Beat It, Childline (2003)

Truancy statistics from DfES, Scottish Executive and National Audit Office

Those Who Bother and Those Who Don't, John Dwyfor Davies and John Lee, (University of West of England, 2006)

Statistics on young people and alcohol, *Guardian*/ICM poll (2007)

Smoking, Drinking and Drug Use among Young People in England, Department of Health (2004)

Report Card 7: an Overview of Child Wellbeing in Rich Countries, J Bradshaw et al. (UNICEF 2007)

Truth Hurts, National Inquiry into Self-harm among Young People (2006)

Putting U in the Picture, Mobile Bullying Survey, NCH/Tesco (2005)

Finally, in writing this book I drew on countless conversations and interviews with experts, which have formed the basis of my work as an education journalist for the last half-dozen years. I am grateful to all those people, too numerous to list, who gave of their time to explain complex things in a way I could understand.

INDEX